SILENCE IS A LETHAL WEAPON

SILENCE IS A LETHAL WEAPON

▼

Surviving Childhood with a Sadistic Pedophile

D. A. Chadwick

Writers Club Press
San Jose New York Lincoln Shanghai

Silence is a Lethal Weapon
Surviving Childhood with a Sadistic Pedophile

Writers Club Press
an imprint of iUniverse.com, Inc.

For information address:
iUniverse.com, Inc.
5220 S 16th, Ste. 200
Lincoln, NE 68512
www.iuniverse.com

This is a work of non-fiction.

ISBN: 0-595-19491-5

Printed in the United States of America

To my late mother, grandmother and brother.
Joyce Marie Chadwick 1939 to 1997
Anna Lillian Erwin 1919 to 1998
Mark Allan Chadwick 1961 to 2000

The three people above all suffered at the hands of my father. I truly hope that there is a better place on the other side as all have more than paid for admission to heaven. This work is also for my aunts and uncles and great grandparents who helped us survive by just being themselves.

Someone told my brother Mark that by bringing up the past I am opening old wounds. If they still bleed, then are not old wounds, are they?

Epigraph

"Our lives begin to end the day we are silent about things that matter."
Dr. Martin Luther King Jr.

Introduction

The following is a true story. It is a sad, painful story, but one that needs to be told and retold until those that choose to rape other people are completey stopped.

Also by D.A. Chadwick
Black Capes and Red Bulls
God Barks
Blatherskites: The Frazer/Gibson Murders
The 1st Field Hospital:The Experiences of T-4 Robert U. Shepard

Contents

List of Tables

Prologue

Background

In the spring of 1998 my brother, Mark, asked me to write our life story. He didn't just ask, he implored. It wasn't anything that I wanted to do. I was working on a mystery novel and really did not want to think about our past, but he insisted that I write it anyway. I compromised by writing a thriller in which the hero, Harry Dolan, hunts down and kills chicken-hawks(pedophiles). I wrote fiction because in real life we received no justice of any kind and I needed to release my increasing anger and frustration with the legal system. Black Capes and Red Bulls is over eighty percent true. The only things not true are; I'm not a guy I wasn't a Ranger in Vietnam and I haven't actually murdered any pedophiles. The names were changed to protect the innocent, not the guilty.

It seems that in this age of enlightenment and legal sophistication that we would no longer have to worry about those that rape children, but alas, pedophiles are going strong. They are also getting louder. There are many child abusers on the Internet who proudly proclaim their "sexual preference" and have elaborate web pages stating that they are "coming out'.

One of the little bullets in their arsenal is a study by Bruce Rind Ph.D known as,' The Rind Study'. The essence of the work is that child sexual abuse can be positive. Yes, you read that right. It is a slap in the face to anyone who has managed to grow to adulthood in spite of these devil's disciples.

I don't know if my father has read it or even heard of it as the only thing he has read that I am aware of is the novel,' The Taking of Pelham One, Two, Three' and a slew of various types of pornography. I cannot bring myself to call him, "Dad" so I'll just call him Al. The Rind Study is just the sort of material that Al used to back up his right to rape his children and Rind certainly is not the first to suggest that maybe sexual abuse is not so bad. Of course, pedophiles the world over are applauding with tears in their eyes that their "preference" is finally being recognized.

When we had to endure family counseling at Menninger's in Topeka, Kansas a similar sentiment was expressed. Mark had suffered more physical abuse that I had and he expressed his anger in violent behavior and problems at school. When he finally ended up at the psychiatric facility, Mark decided that he'd had enough of paying for Al's crimes. Mark wrote the U.S. Army and told them what dear old dad was doing to his children. The look on Al's face when he thought he might actually be treated like a criminal was priceless. Of course, he got out of it by once again going through counseling. Most of the time Mark had violated some rule and was not allowed to be in on the family sessions. My youngest brother and sister were also left out as everyone assumed that Al would not have the gonads to diddle kids while being investigated by the army. This was a very large mistake.

Our regular therapist was on vacation one session and a man took her place. I mention this as I liked our regular therapist, Marianne Roche, and she would never have said such a thing to my mother. The "family" session consisted of me, Mom and Al and we had to sit in a circle knowing that the whole scene was being taped. The counselor announced that in these type of cases(I assume he meant incest) they find that the wife is not willing to fully sexually satisfy her husband, so he turns to his children. I shall never forget the smug look of self satisfaction that crossed Al's face. He sat there pumped up like the chickenhawk that he is and his expression said, "See, I told you it wasn't my fault!" Every part of my body wanted to fly across the room and strangle the pompous bastard right where he sat and maybe that shrink too. I shall also never forget the demoralized look on my mother's face. She did not deserve that remark and I know she ever got over it even though I continually told her it was crap

Those that have read my book Black Capes and Red Bulls have enjoyed it and wanted more Harry Dolan books. I obliged and wrote, God Barks, which also targets another group of humans that I cannot tolerate; racist, narrow-minded, Bible thumping hate-mongers. It is important to me to spread the word about the horrors inflicted by pedophiles and if writing non-fiction is the way to do that in this market, then so be it. There are some who don't like the revenge Dolan takes on his father in Black Capes, but I don't really care. I don't feel like writing gut-wrenching, tear-jerking poetry that makes one want to commit suicide. I hate my father and all the misery he has passed out. It is much better to take out such anger in writing than to load up the shotgun and blow the SOB back to the hell that spawned him.

By sharing my experiences I hope to aid those trying to recover from their own versions of "Al" or those still being victimized. This story is also for the emotionally and mentally or physically abused partner of the child rapist as they choose their mates very carefully. All those sexually abused as children probably remember these excuses;

She/he wets the bed because they are too lazy to get up.

The child wets the bed because their bladder is too small to hold urine all night.

The child sets fires and tortures animals so he must be a sociopath. He's just born that way, nobody caused it.

The child is hyperactive and needs a drug to slow him down.

He acts up in school just because he is brat.

Those tears in the child's rectum came from a large, rough bowl movement

She's just extremely shy, she isn't full of self hatred.

Those kids don't respect their father because they are ingrates who don't appreciate him.

She gets all those urinary track infections because she has some rare kidney disorder.

Chapter One

Our Own Story

Al always told us stories about how he was abused as a child and never said a good word about any member of his family except for his twin brother. I don't know how much is true as Al likes to color things in his favor. He described an incident where a sixteen year old boy molested him in a field and then the teenager threatened to burn his own parents house down if Al told. Al went to his uncle who supposedly laughed at the five year old's tale and when the sixteen year old found out that Al told, he did indeed burn down his parent's house. The woman of the house came running out in flames and dropped to her knees on the front lawn, her features a mass of fire except for a gaping black hole where her mouth cried for help. While this is a horrible story, but I never thought that it made since. I realize now that Al was the sixteen year old and he killed that five year old's parents for ratting on him. There are many types of pedophiles, but the worst are the sadists and those that are smart enough to breed their own victims. Many will state that they were abused as children, which may be true, but it should never be used as an excuse for raping kids. Pedophiles all know how to wrench sympathy from people, even their own victims. Al is what is known as an introverted pedophile. Basically, he doesn't have the guts to target stranger's children so he married and made his own. Like all criminals, he looked for just the right victim to marry and unfortunately, he met my mother, Joyce Erwin.

Mom was very shy with little self esteem. Her father left my grandmother for a waitress he met at a truck stop. Grandma, Anna Erwin, was pregnant with the youngest child when he told her to, " go to work or starve." This took place in the 1940s when it was a social disgrace to be divorced or poor. The Erwin's lived in rural Kansas and Anna had to work herself ragged to support her children, but society has little sympathy for those little money or status. Mom had terrible memories of being laughed at for wearing patched clothes and for being "from the country." She often lay in bed at night in Ingalls, Kansas listening to the trains go by and longed to board one of them on the way to a better life

Allan Chadwick must have seemed pretty harmless at five foot, seven inches and one hundred twenty-five pounds. My mother wrote in her diary that he was shy and I'm sure that was appealing to her. There were signs of his true personality early on, such as exchanging the broken window in his car for the good one from his mother-in-law's and then putting the broken window in hers. Anna worked hard as a waitress then and Al knew that she did not have the money to replace the glass. My mother never knew about that incident or the numerous times he hid money from her even before they were married. There are many characteristics of Al that are common to all criminals. They know how to charm a victim, conceal their more unsavory actions and isolate the victim from their support group. Al was especially good at making sure Joyce Erwin had no where to turn. He began his brow beating in Leadville, Colorado when he worked graveyard shift at the mine in Climax. Mom never talked much about her early life there, but did say that she was terrified to make a sound while he slept and she was too afraid to go downtown by herself. She was miserable enough to consider calling her mother for a bus ticket home. Al must have been really pleased with himself. But a strike at the mine sent them back to El Dorado, Kansas and Joyce's family.

I was born in El Dorado in 1959. At least for her first two children my mother had her family for support. Just when he started to sexually abuse me I don't know, but I was not even a year old when I would cry if placed on his lap and I told my mother before I was two that I was different from the other kids. My grandmother would come pick me up when I cried and he didn't like it . Al would use this story to try and convince me that my grandmother was wicked and trying to break up his family. He also said she was domineering, which is ludicrous. Anna was around five foot and easy going and if she truly had been so over-bearing, Al would have been thrown out on his ass. God, how I wish she had been capable of making him leave. This was the beginning of Al's "everybody is against me" routine

There was little work in Kansas at that time so Al joined the army. He wished that he was ten thousand miles away from the Erwin's and then found himself in Korea. We heard this sob story many times as well as the one about when Mark was born. My mother didn't want Al to worry about her being pregnant and on her own while he was in Korea, so she waited to surprise him with Mark. She did not know that he would have been kept stateside since she was pregnant. Al used this opportunity to say that Mark was not his and Mom had slept with his twin brother. He also tried to make out that Mark had something wrong with the shape of his head and Mom was some kind of bimbo that didn't notice. From the first time that monster laid eyes on Mark he hated him.

Our pleasant times living down the street from grandma and being around my mother's extended family were soon over as Al volunteered for a tour in Okinawa. One way or another, he would get us away from those that cared about us. Our first house in Okinawa was a blue stucco and next to a large tomb. It was here that I remember Al first sexually abusing us and here that Al began to really target Mark for physical abuse. One afternoon I was sitting in his lap on the couch and I felt Al get an erection. I punched him in the throat and he slammed me down so hard on the floor that I nearly broke my toe. Of course, he got all the sympathy because Mom didn't know why I hit him, but Al did.

Al head-hunted for Mark from the time he was born and made out like the boy was evil and trying to come between him and his wife. One day Al took Mark, who was three at the time, for a car ride and wrecked the old Opal . Mom was told some bullshit story, but Mark told me that Al did it on purpose. He had gone down some isolated dead end road and drove right into a brick wall. Car rides with dear old dad would become a nightmare for other reasons later on and that would not be the last time Al would try to kill his children. In the end, he finally put Mark in his grave.

What makes rape in your own home so much worse than rape elsewhere, is that your home is no longer a sanctuary from the cruel world. I dreaded each night and every time my mother left the house and I was only five years old. When I started school we moved to a house on post and I found out that being shorter than everyone else and having curly hair made me a freak. So then I dreaded school and home any time he was there. One day when Mom was away Al made me and Mark strip and get into bed with him. Al was disgusting and had an equally putrid body with an uncut penis. He made Mark suck on it and me as well. Mark told Mom when she returned and she was furious.

It was 1966 then and despite all the stories about the sixties and free love, society was very closed mouthed about child abuse, incest and divorce. Joyce was, by her own admission, very naive about sex and life in general. Al told her his pathetic childhood stories and was made to go to counseling. Okinawa was the first place that I saw Al use his crying routine. He would get on his knees and while bawling and wailing hobble his way over to my mother, who as a kind person, could not ignore his suffering. As I grew older and met other people in similar situations I discovered that this routine is common among losers in general. The U.S. Army choose not to do anything about Allan Chadwick then nor would it ever. I remember standing on the playground when I was six and wondering if life would ever get any better. It was a good thing that I did not know the answer as I would have thrown myself in front of a truck. The next assignment was Falls Church, Virginia. It was here that we learned of the still lingering hatred that southerners have for Yankees and things would get much worse with Al as he now had the Pentagon to back him up. Al had a free ticket to treat his wife and children anyway he felt like treating them and he took advantage of it. In Virginia Al decided to let his full sadistic personality reign. It is impossible to write down every wicked action as Al went out of his way to make life a dreaded misery. Al had decided to take up drinking at the enlisted club after work, which introduced us to a whole new brand of Hell. Nearly every dinner time was a lesson in cruelty and usually ended with me being mad, Mom crying and Mark getting beat with a belt for refusing to eat chicken or roast beef. The times Al didn't get physical he would pick someone to make fun of or to criticize, usually one of us. You also have to imagine the screaming and cussing Al was doing while trying to force Mark to eat. The reddened face and bulging veins in Al's head made him look like some demon on a rampage. He was never happy unless everyone in the house was either crying or planning to murder him.

As children, me and Mark spent much of the time playing far away from the house because of Al. When he wasn't there we enjoyed being around Mom who went out of her way to make cookies, drew things for us to color and was bright and happy-everything he was not. In 1967 my great-grandfather died. He was our only real grandfather figure as we hated Al's father. I was proud of the fact that Andy Lawless had been a town Marshall and worked as powderman for the railroad, but Al would take every opportunity to run him down. The only happy times I really knew were when we went to visit relatives in Kansas, which meant either Christmas, summer time or a funeral. Great grandpa died on Mark's birthday, July 21. It truly felt like God was on Al's side and hated us as much as Al did. Ironically, I didn't want to go to church with Mom as I thought God was a jerk, so me and Mark stayed home with Al. He made us regret it, as well as any time that we would come home from playing to find Mom at the store or PTA meeting. Al was very fond of orgy type scenarios and individual sessions too. Every perverted act he saw in a porno magazine, Al tried on us. Allan Chadwick could turn anything in life into the vile and disgusting

Looking back on those years I can see clearly how Al manipulated all of us. I've worked in law enforcement and social services and I've seen the same patterns of child and spouse abuse over and over again. In a way, it is comforting to know that there are others out there who have suffered the same way, yet it is sickening to know that too.

When we moved to Falls Church in 1967 we lived in a place called Tyler Gardens. It was where the poor people lived and there were those at school who would not let us forget that or the fact that our father was in the army when things were heating up in Vietnam. School was a nightmare for Mark and myself. Mark was dyslexic, but that disorder was not recognized then and he was just seen as a "bad boy". Around this time Mark began to set fires and be mean to small animals. When Mark told a counselor at school that we were being sexually abused at home, the army rushed to his aid and Al's only punishment was sessions with a shrink. As usual, while conning a therapist with his boo hoo tales from childhood, Al was raping his son and daughter at home. My mother was told it was her duty to stay with her husband and support him in his time of need. It always amazed me how much more important Allan Chadwick was than his wife and kids. He was attached to the CIA at this point and could do no wrong. The activities that Al did in Vietnam were classified, but I managed to find out that he "extracted information from prisoners." He was good at physical and mental torture because he fined tuned his interrogator skills on his family

School was full of taunts, fights and trips to the principal's office, even for me. Those that tormented us on the playground or threw me over a fence to land on walnuts were never punished. Mark would beat up those who picked on me or just plain hit me for the hell of it. There is no such thing as southern hospitality, unless you are just passing through and spending money. You are not invited to stay. They called us Yankees and really believed that we still had Indian problems in Kansas. My teacher in the fourth grade had a heavy Boston accent and didn't like girls. She really helped my feelings of self worth when she down played everything I did because I lacked a penis. I guess being a tomboy wasn't close enough. Right before we went to Okinawa we were stationed in New Jersey for a time. While there I developed a Jersey accent in which I did not pronounce ' r ', so Madison Elementary put me in speech class. It didn't seem fair to me that Mrs. Snell could butcher the English language and be hired as a teacher and I had to be in a "special" class to correct a very similar accent.

The walk home was just as bad. I dreaded seeing anyone my own age standing on a corner as it only meant more torment. As soon as we got home me and Mark would change into play clothes and head out to ride our bikes around the neighborhood. Of course, Tyler Gardens had more that its share of bullies and future serial killers and we seemed to run into them all. The worst of the bunch was a blond haired boy named Joey Castor. He ran around with a group of flunkies who did whatever he told them to do. On one occasion me and Mark were caught off by ourselves near a creek that ran into a culvert. Joey and his cronies tied Mark to a post and then threw him down into the hole while sitting on me. I was dirty and Mark's clothes were tore. Instead of being mad at the bullies like most fathers would, Al sided with Castor and we were punished for ruining our clothes. I never said, " I'll call my dad!" to other children as I knew that Al would always side with the others against his wife and kids. I truly hope Joey Castor had a miserable life, but he probably became a Republican or a malpractice lawyer or both.

The first townhouse we had at Tyler Gardens was just a two bedroom and in 1968 we finally came up on the list for a three bedroom. One of the bedrooms was really a walk-in closet and it was to be my room with part of Mark's room used as a playroom for us both. This place had a larger yard and we wanted a dog. Other people had them so I thought it strange that Al said the manager didn't allow dogs. He said that he would ask if dogs were allowed and made a big production of it knowing that his children were very excited about it. We waited for over an hour in the car while Al talked with the manager. When he finally emerged Al wore the frown that he always wore, which looked like an upside down horseshoe. Mark dubbed this expression," the hemorrhoid look", because it usually preceded asinine behavior. Even Mom was anxious by his time and eager to hear what the man had said. Al got in the car and remained silent until Mom asked him to speak up, then he said the manager said no dogs. After letting me and Mark be upset for several minutes, Al then added, unless we have a fenced yard. We finally went to a pet store and bought a Pekinese we named Patrick D. Mack that was nearly as much of an asshole as our father. Al tried to make every aspect of our young lives unhappy. A trip to get ice cream was no exception. He would announce that we were all getting vanilla cones and Mom would say that she wanted a malt. Al would harass her until she cried and gave in.

For some reason Al stopped bothering me sexually for a few weeks. He still ran me down and made fun of everything I was good at, but he let up on abusing me. It certainly did not hurt my feelings any. What child wants to learn the '69' position from their own father? I noticed that he would march past my room to Mark's to say goodnight, so I made a comment on it. Al corrected this omission and resumed his wee hour visits. My mother never had a decent nights sleep as she was always listening to hear how long Al's trips to the bathroom were lasting. Every fourth or fifth night though, Mom would be worn out and sleep all night and Al would creep through the house like pus draining from a wound.

In December of 1968 Mom became pregnant for the third time with our brother, Andy.. She was thrilled, but Al wasn't. I have never understood why he didn't want more children as he was a stone cold pedophile and his two oldest kids were getting past his age of interest. Mom went on a field trip with my class when she was around seven months into the pregnancy. She had to walk home as we only had one car at that time and Al had it parked at the Pentagon. I remember watching her walk away from the school in her dress and a light coat and I felt so sorry for her. She had no one when she should have had a husband to share in the joy of a new child-there was only Al's anger and cruelty and depravity. Mom tried so hard to bring light and happiness into our lives and he went out of his way to paint everything in infected hues. On August 25, 1969 we were awakened by our parents in the middle of the night. Mom was in labor and we all piled into the station wagon for the trip to the hospital at Fort Belvior. Once we knew that we had a new baby brother, Al brought Mark and me home "to sleep". While Mom was in the hospital with a new baby Al made his other two children have an orgy with him. Neither one of us ever told Mom. It was too horrible to fathom, much less talk about. It should have been a time of joy. I still have a problem believing in a God that puts a woman like Joyce Erwin together with a wretched being like Allan Chadwick. I am inclined to think the Cathars were right about the physical world belonging to Rex Mundi and God has little to do with it. Pedophiles have to be Satan's crowning glory.

Shortly after the arrival of Andy, we moved to Independence Hill just outside of Manassas, Virginia. There were several houses there left from an old air force base that the army still used. We lived across the street from an old Civil War graveyard and two abandoned churches. It was here that I learned to love history. The houses were surrounded by forest which was both good and bad for Mark and me. We could play in the woods for hours and never see Al, but again, the woods were an excellent place for Al to become more sadistic. Mark began to strangle kittens in the woods and saw various shrinks for this behavior and was put on medication. It was not until 1998 that Mark told me Al showed him how to strangle cats while masturbating. I was shocked. Mom and me had assumed that Mark was acting out, but it had not occurred to me that our father taught him that sickening act.

Life became unbearable at Independence Hill. It did not help that once again the locals hated the military. I would like to see military service be mandatory for everyone as defending the country is not the problem of just a few. It is not right that so many didn't mind taking our money and then treated us like trash. Al's drinking must have increased as he out did himself in screaming, cussing, degrading us and Mark's physical abuse increased. We weren't even safe when visiting grandma as Al pushed Mark up against the heater in the bathroom and burned his buttocks. Of course, he claimed it was an accident. I recall how bad my grandmother felt about having that type of heater in the bathroom and Al just let her take the guilt.

When I went to junior high in Manassas I was miserable. I hated gym class and was terrible at gymnastics. One Wednesday I had a full day of humiliation and I was laying bed dreading the next day. Sometime after midnight I heard the door to my bedroom creak open. I knew it was Al and told him that if he touched me again I would kill him, then I told him to get the hell out. He ceased to sexually abuse me, but turned his talents to mental and emotional abuse.

Al's hatred of Mark seemed to increase by the month. While Mom would decorate the house for holidays bright and cheery, Al would come along and push over the Christmas tree or some other act of disrespect and find some reason to take a belt to Mark. He would chase Mark around his room and we could hear furniture being turned over and Mark screaming. Mom would rush in to stop it and to this day I don't know why Al never hit Mom or he just didn't do it in front of us. I know that he did something to her as numerous times she would sit by the phone crying, desperately wanting to call her mother and sister for help, but did not. Al told me that if I tried to "get him" that he would tell the cops and the army that the sexual abuse was all Mom's idea and he would put her in jail. He said, " Who do you think they will believe? Me or some ignorant country girl?" I had seen this scum of the earth get away with rape for ten years and had no reason to doubt that he could twist things around and make Mom do the prison time. While Mark received generous portions of Al's regards physically, I was torn down mentally and emotionally. Everything that I loved to do and was good at, Al tore apart. My writing, music and art were all worthless and I was around twelve years old when he first called me," Jack of All Trades and Master of None". This was an insult that he used up until 1997 when I stopped seeing him or talking to him-the year Mom died of cancer. Unfortunately, Mark began to take out some of his anger on Andy who was a toddler. Later, Mark told me that he was mad at Andy because he truly believed that Al favored him and had not abused him. Al made Mark feel like a piece of trash and he didn't understand why Andy was so much better and thus, abuse free. We were all wrong.

Fall of 1970 Mom was pregnant again. I once asked her how she could have sex with Al and she told me that she thought that it would keep him off of us. She truly meant well, but we did not have a real understanding of pedophiles then. Pedophiles like to rape children, period. Mark's problems were escalating, so instead of volunteering for TDY(temporary duty) as Al usually did when he wanted to dump all the troubles on Mom, Al chose Vietnam. For one whole year we had no predator living with us, but he still managed to hurt us along distance. I find it disturbing that neither me or Mark remember anything about the year that Mom was pregnant with Lisa. Why would we have such vivid memories of everything else? Mark was concerned about what could have happened that we would both block it out. I was in the seventh grade, Mark the fifth, Andy was two and Lisa a few months old when we returned to El Dorado, Kansas in 1971. We lived in a three bedroom house within site of my aunt and uncle's house. Mark told me shortly before he died in May 2000 that it was the best year of his childhood. At least for a time we saw grandma and had family gatherings like everyone else. Even though Mom's family meant very much to her, if was difficult to shake off Al's influence. He had worked on us all for years trying to turn us against my mother's family and the only reason it didn't work on me and Mark is we hated Al and had no bond with him at all. Through the years I have tried to figure out why Mom didn't just tell her sister everything that year, but she didn't. Of course, Mark and me didn't either, which I regret terribly. Mom wrote to Al every day and he sent back some wicked letters to her. One in particular was so bad she didn't write back for several weeks and he responded by not sending us any money for the month of December. I have included a letter as an example of the type of manipulation criminals and abusers use to keep people beaten down and under their control. Al claimed to have received only a few letters from Mom, but I know better. You cannot send over three hundred letters to someone and have only a handful reach them, not even in a war zone. He was at Camp Eagle the whole time, so I'm sure Al read most of the five page letters Mom wrote daily. She told him about how Andy and Lisa were advancing and what Mark and me were doing in school. I remember watching her cramp her hands writing to him and thinking, what a waste of time. Al denied cheating on Mom over there, but that isn't the same story he told the chief of detectives in El Dorado after she died. Of course, I never believed that Al went for a whole year without sex of any kind-not possible. You will notice how typically self serving this letter is and how Al always has to out do everyone else even in suffering.

Letter from Al to his wife date February 1972

"I received one letter from you today. I was so glad to get it. Without your letters life would be miserable. I'm so glad you read my letter to Debbie and Mark. I felt that they should know that they didn't do anything bad. I felt so bad about having to put that in a letter instead of telling it to you. It's not your fault I went off the deep end. I read somewhere that when someone goes off like that it always the ones they love that get hurt. I don't want you blaming yourself for it. I don't want Deb and Mark blaming themselves either.

You said you felt like you had lived a hundred years. I know how you feel, except I felt like I had died a million times and just woke up to find myself alone. Once when we were talking about having grey hair and I said that you had more and you jokingly said that I put them there. That hurt me so much because I knew it was true. I had put them there. If my childhood had been different I would have been prepared to share my family with my in-laws. I saw my father live in the same town with his grandchildren and never go visit them. I saw things taken from me that to me were very important. I was forced to give up my mother and the same night heard my father say, "I don't believe she ever loved me", so you see you had nothing to do with that.

I can remember things now that were impossible for me to remember before. Little things come back to me at the oddest times. Things I didn't want to remember before because of what they reminded me of . One of those things was the day we brought Debbie home to your mother's house. It was a mess and needed cleaned up. You bathed her on the table with all of that junk still on it. Well, that reminded me of my childhood and scared me to see her there in the midst of what to me was my childhood. In short, I didn't want her there because of what it reminded me of. Another time that carries back to me was your mother holding Deb in the rocker while you was sleeping. I wanted to hold her so bad it hurt, but I didn't want to just grab her away from mom. I can now remember that terrible feeling. I was just afraid she would never give her back. Now I can remember what she looked like. I can see her eyes looking up at me and watching me. When things like that came back to me it puts tears in my eyes and I get close to losing control of my emotions. It's almost like seeing your baby for the first time after being blind. I told you one time that I didn't remember her first year. Well, piece by piece it's coming back.

I should be thankful that they have a grandmother who loves and cherishes them. I know that their grandfather doesn't cherish his own children much less his grandchildren. Mark has paid debts he didn't owe. I remember when I told him he was a problem child. How blind was I? It was me who was the problem. I was insanely jealous of a little boy who wasn't even old enough to tie his shoes. When he was laying in that bed at McConnell I thought that God was going to take him from me for being like I was. I know how much he loves me and I am ashamed of myself for not accepting him. I just hope they can forgive me and give me the chance to be the real father. Well, I'll close for now. Love Daddy."

Before anyone gets to shedding big tears for poor Al, let me point out a few things. My grandmother worked long hours and her house may have been cluttered, but never has Anna Erwin ever been dirty. I was the first grandchild and niece, so it isn't so surprising that my grandmother and aunt were excited by my presence. Another reason that grandma was so eager to scoop me up was that Al was mean to me whenever Mom left the room or house. He goes on and on about not remembering things, but I don't know who he was trying to fool. All I heard about for the first ten years of my life was horror stories from Al's childhood and lies about what my aunt and grandmother did to break up his "happy family". Al's concern for Mark is entirely self serving and he must have forgotten his high regard for Mark when he threw him into the street in March 2000. When Al referred to seeing Mark in a hospital bed at McConnell air force base it was because Mark had been diagnosed with juvenile diabetes and the only reason Mark got to see a doctor was my mother nearly exploded with anger. That summer before Daddy of the Year went to Vietnam, Mark kept getting sicker and more run down. When Mom wanted to take him to a doctor, Al refused. It was only due to Mom saying she was taking him to McConnell with or without Al that Mark didn't die that summer. I'm sure that was our father's intention. The Chadwick family is riddled with diabetes and I know that Al knew exactly what Mark's symptom's meant.

I prayed nightly that Al would die in Vietnam. The idea of moving again made me sick and I tried to find ways to stay behind, including living with grandma or attending a boarding school. The day we had to go pick him up at the airport had to be one of the most demoralizing days of my life. When I saw him in khakis with the ribbons the army stuck on him I wanted to puke. Al has the coldest, lizard-like eyes you could ever see and his frowning face made me want to either shoot him or me. My aunt and grandmother were with us and my aunt still recalls the strange, distant way they greeted each other. Why Al ever came back from Vietnam is something I would like to know. He hated all of us and had a whole country full of orphans to abuse, so why did he come back? Al simply liked to make people miserable. The next assignment was Fort Bragg, North Carolina. We lived in a trailer house off base until housing could open up on post. I remember laying in bed and feeling desolate and hopeless and knowing that Al hadn't changed any. When Andy and Lisa were babies and Mom was out I would never let Al change their diapers or give them bathes. We all continued to watch Al like a hawk around the little ones. If I had known then what I do now, I would have killed my father when I was still a juvenile and saved everyone a good deal of misery.

Our school experiences were not great and I went to the worst high school there was in Fayettevile, North Carolina, E.E. Smith. It was so bad that parents had to draw names from a bowl to select one of the three area high schools. Mom really dreaded telling me what school she had drawn. To my great shame I was still wetting the bed, which is a common behavior in abused children. Mom did not know what else to do as doctor's said it was just me, so she said that I couldn't join the horseback riding club if I didn't stop. I stopped wetting the bed all right, but have suffered from insomnia ever since then. Al must have developed sneakier ways of diddling kids as we never suspected that he was stupid enough to start on Andy, but he had. There was also a string of rapes one summer in our area where someone came in through a window at night and raped a six month old, an eighteen month old and a one year old. Of course, all made bad witnesses and the rapist was not caught, but Al worked the night shift then and I seriously wonder if he did it.

Mark began breaking and entering and drug use at Fort Bragg. He made no effort to conceal his crimes, yet nothing was ever done about it. We were followed by suits in government cars who took pictures of Mark and me walking to school, our mail was censored and the phone tapped. The CIA even opened letters from my great grandmother! The only thing Al every got into trouble for in the army was when Mom wrote to the Chinese embassy for information on the MIA whose bracelet I wore. Sgt. Chadwick came home all flustered and pissed off because he had to answer for Mom's actions. You can't write foreign governments or be gay in the military, but if you'd rather lick a child's sexual organ instead of a pop sickle, that's okay!

The summer of 1976 Al received orders for Virginia again. It was too expensive to live out there so it was decided that we would return to Kansas and Al would go to Virginia alone. At that time the real estate market was very tight and there were only two houses for sale big enough for us or worth buying. The house on Race Street needed major remodeling and an up stairs built and it was a sheer delight working with Al. For most of my high school years the house was under construction. Mom was thrilled to finally own a house, but Al cut whatever corners he could and it was obvious that he could care less about the house. Mark's violent behavior increased and he was picked on in El Dorado as well as every other place we had lived. For people that are so concerned about the shootings going on in high schools today, heed this bit of advice. All those that have gunned down fellow students and teachers have said the same things-that they were picked on and made fun of in school. I know from my own experience and Mark's that there are too many teachers, coaches and principals that look the other way when certain students are being tormented. In days past the less popular students either dropped out or spent their high schools days taking the abuse, but for some reason they are not doing that anymore. No one has the right to ruin someone else's existence and society needs to quit saying it is all right for the good looking, the rich or the athletically inclined to hound another child to desperation.

Once when Mark was in the Butler county jail, a large deputy punched him in the face while he was handcuffed. Mark was sixteen and the cop was not fired, but promoted. The year Al was in Virginia, Mom had a very rough time with Mark and as usual Al managed to not have to deal with the mess he made. Mark broke into the El Dorado library and a grade school with a friend and did considerable amount of damage. He was placed on probation, but soon violated it and was sent to a group home in Wichita. The manager of the home was also a chaplain in the Sedgwick County Sheriff's Department. While there Mark told the man what Al had done to us and feared for his youngest brother and sister, but once again it was not deemed necessary for Allan Chadwick to pay for his crimes or be removed from the house. Mark nearly killed another boy while in Wichita and was then sent to The Menninger Foundation in Topeka. Around 1977 was when Mark contacted the army from the psychiatric hospital. He wasn't getting any better and just wanted out. Shortly after that Mark was sent home. Al could have been sent to Leavenworth and Al could not tolerate being labeled a child molester. I was attending Kansas University at that time, but dropped out because I had to work full time and my car would not run. Al said there was nothing wrong with it, but it was another way to ensure that none of his children were more successful than himself. Mark returned home, but soon lived with a friend's family to get away from Al.

The next decade found Mark in Boston and I ended up in California after a brief stint in the army. The Army rushed to discharge me for not lying about my sexuality in 1983 ,which was laughable. I scored high on all the tests, was a good shot and could do fifty pushups when I arrived at Fort Dix. My only fault was that I did not want to lie about being gay, but we can't have fairies in the military. The only beings with wings allowed in the service are chickenhawks! In 1979 I was hit by a drunk driver on my birthday. Mark and I had gone to see the movie,' Halloween', and a guy from Bethel college(who was not supposed to consume alcohol while a student there)plowed into us when he ran a red light at fifty miles an hour. My knee was tore up and then butchered even more by an incompetent surgeon who did not notice that I also had a broken ankle. The same knee took another blow when the pavement fell out from under my patrol car one rainy California night when I was responding to an alarm at the Santa Paula airport. Eventually, this accident brought me back to Kansas in 1987.

The summer of 1987 we found out that my younger brother was also abused. Al had simply changed tactics and was more subtle and sneaky. Andy thought we were at family counseling at Menninger's for what happened to him and was surprised to know that Al had sexually abused his oldest sister and brother. Mom was devastated and told Al to pack his bags, that he wasn't wanted there any longer. Al simply got red faced and stormed into the living room while telling us all that we needed to calm down. While Mom and Andy comforted each other, Lisa looked into the living room and told me to come look too. There Al was sitting in his chair smoking a cigarette, tapping his foot and looking very smug and self satisfied. We knew that he wasn't going anywhere. I don't know what he said or did to my mother, but Al got away with talking to a shrink again.

Later that summer my grandmother was raped for two hours in the middle of the night in her own house. The rapist knew where everything in her house was, including the tape and cotton balls that he placed over her eyes. He took his sweet time while saying rude things to her then went through her drawers and purse commenting on her economic status. A witness who was walking down the street that night saw a man smoking a cigarette on the porch. The ribbing had been pulled on a bedroom window off the porch so the cops figured the intruder came through that window, but I never did think he did. There was a wide dresser in front of the window full of ceramic figures that no one could have stepped over without falling or knocking the fragile items off.

The only cop that thought the rapist was known to Anna Erwin, drowned before he could investigate the case. If the cops had questioned us about that night the case could have been solved that month. The night grandma was raped was very strange indeed. None of us heard the police pounding on the door the first time. They had to call my aunt and say we were not home. She sent them back as she knew that Mom was there. When they returned, Andy finally heard the doorbell ring and answered the front door in his underwear, something that he would not normally do. No one is our family slept sound except for the old predator himself. It is very odd that me, Mom and Andy did not hear police shouting and banging on the door.

Another odd thing was the location of the phone. Lisa was spending the night at a friend's house, so Mom had placed the old fashion table phone(we didn't have wireless then) on a table outside her bedroom door in case something should happen to Lisa. The phone had been moved around the corner near the bathroom and a blanket piled on top of it. Stranger still, I was asleep in the basement and did not hear any of the commotion with the cops or the conversations up stairs. Only when Andy shouted downstairs that grandma had been raped did I hear anything at all and I had a difficult time waking up. We were all in deep shock and hurriedly dressed for the trip to the hospital. Al was working second shift then and had been doing over time after midnight, but it didn't mean anything at the time. He was standing in the middle of the kitchen fully dressed and all hunched into himself, shivering like a little boy in trouble. I didn't think anything of it then as Al was fruitcake anyway.

It is a terrible thing to see your grandmother a short time after some piece of garbage raped and degraded her in her own bed. He threatened her with a knife and told her not to look at him, then went through out the house gathering tape and cotton balls to cover her eyes. The rapist had taken the fan out of her window to stop sound from carrying outside. Once he had her eyes bound tightly shut the man felt confident enough to turn on lights in the house. He told Anna that he could tell she was a poor woman from the jewelry she owned. The rapist said rude, demeaning things to her knowing that grandma had not had sex in decades. When he tried to make her do oral sex she cried and the scumbag didn't make her do it. He left and told her not to call the police.

What made this event even harder to take was my aunt and uncle lived just one house away. Grandma ran down the street to her daughter's house for help. At first my aunt didn't know what she was saying and the mess of tape around her head looked like a contraption that grandma might wear with curlers. It was very hard for Anna to tell the police and her family what the bastard had done. She was sixty-eight years old at the time and grandma was never the same again. Anna aged more rapidly after that night and she never again opened her windows. For two months I stayed with her in the room where the rapist supposedly came through the window. I lay there with a loaded Smith and Wesson .357 Magnum hoping the asshole would return as I knew that some rapists do. Al got his revenge in the worst way he could have and he showed us all that he would have his own way-no one tells him to pack his bags.

It wasn't until after my mother died that we started to put all the pieces together. We all had been just going to ignore Al, especially me and Lisa as Al had been mean to Mom when she had her heart attack in 1993 and down right cruel when she was diagnosed with cancer. I tell this story more fully in Black Capes and Red Bulls. We found pictures of JonBenet Ramsey in Al's dresser drawer along with tubes of K-Y Jelly and pornography magazines with photographs of shaved women that looked like very young girls. While Mom was dying in the living room, Al had been masturbating to pictures of a murdered, sexually abused little girl. This discovery brought back many unwanted memories and something Al said made us rethink the night of grandma's rape.

I remember how furious Mom had been that the phone was moved, but neither Andy or I had done it. Why would we? Al made the statement to Mark after Mom died that the El Dorado Police were stupid for not running the print on the masking tape the rapist used on grandma's face. It was a real blow to hear him say such a thing. No one remembered that the rapist had used masking tape and the police had to pull the old file to verify it. Then I remembered that the key to grandma's front door had been lost years ago and it was assumed that a grandchild had taken it outside. I know now that Al used the key to go through the front door that night and it also explains how a rapist could know where everything in Anna Erwin's house was located. Al moved the phone so we never heard the police dispatcher or my aunt calling. He did not work overtime that night at Beechcraft. I fully believe that he put something in our drinks that night to make us sleep like rocks. Of course, the statue of limitations was nearly up and nothing was done to Allan Chadwick once again.

Mark came to live with me in 1998 to die among family. The juvenile diabetes had really taken its toll on him. In 1995 Mark had open heart surgery, but he was not able to return to work as a medical technician near Boston. He wanted to die in our mother's house, so he moved in with Al in 1999. Mark was also concerned about a neighbor boy who spent too much time alone with Al and had to be bodily thrown from the house when he didn't get his candy and cookies. We all knew what had been happening to that child for a year. Most of this story is told in the Harry Dolan book, God Barks, but what I want to mention here is what Al did to his dying son.

To make a long, disgusting story short, Mark was supposed to get out of the house so Al could sell it. Al had a stroke in August of 1999 and was sent to Oklahoma to live with a niece. On Friday March 3, 2000, Mark returned home from dialysis to find Al and a herd of his cronies there with the police. For those unfamiliar with the rigors of hemodialysis, this was a very chickenshit act. He was also a double amputee who had to roll from the handicapped bus into this crowd of cold blooded hypocrites. They had trashed the house and crammed what little they thought Mark needed into boxes. Al knew that Mark was moving out, but his house was not ready yet. My friend, Joyce Akins, bought him a little one bedroom house to live in as Mark could not afford to live anywhere in El Dorado on his disability The eviction squad was aware that the house needed major remodeling and that my house was not wheelchair accessible, but they told the cops that they had made arrangements for Mark to live with me. That was interesting, since I had not spoken to most of those present at the shunning for months, especially Al. I told the cop who came to my door the situation and he said that they could not throw Mark on the curb. So Al had to pay for two whole nights in a motel room. Mark called me and told me what was happening and to not come over as I would be arrested. I had no doubt that Al, my sperm donor, would have done just that

I cannot say enough good about my aunt and uncle, Jim and Phyllis Anderson. I always knew my aunt was a strong ally and she came through for us. She went to Mark's motel room that night while the gestapo was still there dumping his stuff in the hot room and endured the insults and lies hurled at her. While Mark was crying on the bed, with no legs and exhausted from dialysis, that bunch went over to a restaurant called the Golden Corral and actually had a victory dinner. They don't realize how such actions get around in a small town and how unpopular it was with many people. Later, they did drop off a box full of Mark's frozen seafood, but he didn't want to call anyone that late at night to come and get it, so it ended up in the trash. Even though the restaurant was next to the motel, they brought Mark nothing to eat. In fact, Al's niece actually had the audacity to tell Mark before they left, "We love you, Mark." It must have been right after a similar situation that someone first uttered the words, "Christ on a Crutch!" Al must be very proud of himself now. That night Mark suffered the first of four heart attacks. Six weeks later he died from a massive heart attack at Via Christi's Saint Joseph campus. Mark had written his own obituary some weeks before and excluded everyone that had turned their backs on him. Incredible as it may seem, Al actually called the funeral home and tried to have the obituary changed to mention him as Mark's father! While Mark shopped at the Salvation Army, Al refused to help him in any way. Of course, just when you think Al cannot out do himself, he reaches up his grimy sleeve and puts out yet another cockroach. Three weeks after Mark died, Al tried to have himself made the beneficiary of Mark's burial policy.

I should backtrack to a few months before Mark died. Al called the insurance company while Mark was at dialysis and made himself the beneficiary of the burial policy that Mom had bought before Mark became a diabetic. Fortunately, we discovered this illegal act and corrected it. We are not talking about a large life insurance policy, but a six thousand dollar burial policy. Since Joyce Akins had used her retirement money from the school system to buy Mark's house, he left his life insurance to her so that she could replace the money in her retirement fund. There was only a little over three thousand dollars after the funeral home bill, but Al kept up the fight. This little act of greed caused four months of problems and the expense of a lawyer, not to the mention the aggravation of the funeral home. We had warned them that Al might cause trouble and he was true to form. The staff at the funeral home said that they had never heard of anyone trying to change the beneficiary after someone died-they had just not dealt with Allan Chadwick in his full glory! Six months after Mark died, Al placed a headstone at the foot of Mom's grave declaring that Mark was a beloved son and brother. Mark was cremated and is not there and I can tell you what sort of colorful things he would have to say about that mammoth hypocritical act. I would like to say there was a happy ending here or that we have seen some justice, but we have not. Allan Chadwick now has three of the people he hated most in life in the ground and he still lives with that niece who cares for small children with Al in the house. As long as Al can move even one finger he is a threat to children and anyone who has their children around him should go to jail

The stories I have told regarding Al's actions are to illustrate that sadistic pedophiles marry solely to produce victims and no other reason. Al's callous acts are typical of criminals with no conscious. This is a guide book to stop the Al's of the world and there are many of them. We need to learn from each other's experiences and unite against those that think children are handy little pieces of meat for them to enjoy without fear of prison time. For those that do not believe that I need to keep telling this story, think about this; Al has no criminal record so if he wished to do so, he could teach, work at a daycare, be a scout leader, coach a baseball team or do any other thing he wants to because the law refuses to stop him. As far as the legal system is concerned Al is Mr. Lily White and a citizen above reproach. Still think that we do not have a problem?

When Al volunteered to do fire walks at the daycare and deliver Meals On Wheels, we knew that something had to be done. It is a little known fact that pedophiles will sometimes turn to the elderly when denied access to children, but I have seen it happen. Old people are basically helpless, weak, easy to scare and many have not had sexual relations in years, so they are kind of like children. Al did not have good intentions when he took meals to shut-ins. Since he had no criminal record we decided to make posters and tell everyone in town that Al is a pedophile. We placed the posters on churches, day cares, stores, car dealers and the senior center where Al had been hanging out. The cops did not like it and told us via my aunt to stop it. For our own safety….. right. Many people have come up to me and thanked me for telling them the truth, especially those that knew Mom. My mother was very well liked and taught at the First Baptist Day Care for sixteen years-Al fully planned to use her good reputation to be allowed around children and avoid suspicion. He pulled the old, " I'll kill myself", routine and checked into a psychiatric hospital. It was not the usual vacation Al enjoyed in hospitals, however, as he spent eight days in lock down. He was also stressed at not being allowed to see his grandchildren, so Al produced a grimy piece of paper to prove his innocence. The document that he took to the police, sent my aunt and gave my siblings was the most wretched piece of forgery I have ever seen. Al claimed to have paid four hundred dollars for a lie detector test in Wichita, Kansas and the company on the letterhead does exist, but the document was a mess. It was a very bad copy, filled with mistakes and there were only two questions on the test;

Did you touch T____peter? Al responds with no

Did you touch B_____pussy? Al responds with no

I do not have a high regard for lie detector tests anyway as Al has passed them his entire life, but any cop that was impressed with that mess should be fired immediately. There were no control questions at all, just the two questions above that use terminology that I seriously doubt any investigator used. Of course, he passed and proudly showed the results to his youngest son and the police. The only reason that Al is not a major threat to children in the area is that he has had several strokes and is now in a wheelchair and unable to speak clearly. I still believe that as long as Al can move one finger he should not be around children, but there are those in this world that believe strokes cure pedophilia. Having a great deal of money aids in the cure as well.

Chapter Two

The Partner of the Abuser

The reality of life is that family members do worst things to each other and more often than any kidnaper or serial killer. Your chances of being beat to death by your own spouse or parent is many times higher than if a stranger were to do it. Why is this so, even at the dawn of the twenty-first century? Despite all the equal rights movements and advanced level of education enjoyed by millions, there is still a reluctance to become involved in another person's problems and many that still believe that a man has the right to discipline his wife. It is difficult to undo a philosophy that has been taught for hundreds of centuries, but undo it we must.

No one intends to marry or live with an abuser. Abusers are criminals and like all criminals they know how to manipulate people for their benefit. Many are sweet and charming to everyone except their own family, thus often victims are not believed when they tell someone they are being mistreated. Domestic crime knows no financial or educational boundaries. Those that wear suits and carry brief cases can be just as violent as the man that operates a jack hammer.

While abusers come in all shapes and sizes they also have many common traits. To avoid being trapped in a bad domestic situation watch out for the following signs in the people you date;

1. They may go over board with the presents and charming gestures. This does not mean that buying gifts for a sweetheart is bad, just be cautious.
2. Jealousy in small amounts may be cute, but jealousy generally indicates a person with little self confidence.

3. While it is natural for couples who just meet to spend time alone, watch out for those that do not like your friends and family and do all they can to keep you away from them. 4. Avoid anyone that solves problems with his fists and has a temper that he makes no effort to control.

5. Not everyone likes children or small animals, but those that think poorly of them are usually masking a deeper problem.
6. If someone you date doesn't want children and you do, then do not become involved with them, especially if you already have children.
7. While compassion is one of the traits that makes us human, be suspect of anyone who immediately begins to tell you horror stories about their childhood or past relationships. Do not play the role of rescuer. Romantic relationships do not solve psychological problems. 8. Do not become involved with someone to solve a financial hardship
9. Do not become involved if you plan on changing that person. If you don't like them as they are, then back off.

10. If you have a job that you enjoy and the person you date expects you to compromise that job for them or their career, then that is not the person for you. Do not give up your hope and dreams for anyone.

So what happens if you find yourself with a controlling abuser anyway? The first question is this, do you have children that need protected? If the answer is yes, then you must take action. Most abusers rely on the fact that you keep silent and have no support group. In some states the laws are written so that a woman has no choice but to leave the situation or face charges for endangering her children. It helps to get the blame off the abused spouse for ending a bad relationship and removes children from poor environments. It is not easy to change your life style or end a relationship no matter how bad it is and some people are involved with extremely violent partners and must hide in shelters to get away. It does not seem fair that the victims are the ones that must leave behind their homes and possessions, but often the victim gets the short end of the stick. You must ask yourself how long you wish to live in good health or in some cases, live at all?

There are abusers who do not leave physical marks, but make no mistake about the devastating effects of mental and emotional abuse. Years of humiliation and criticism will break a person down and they will not even know it. Abusers like to control people and they will do two things to accomplish this task. First they will eliminate your outside contacts with family and friends, then they will made you feel worthless and unable to function without them. Abusive partners will convince you that your family is against you and wants only to break up your happy relationship because they don't want what is best for you. Unless your blood family are the ones abusing you, do not side with a sexual partner against your family. Relationships can be dissolved, but blood relatives cannot. If your friends and family do not like the person you are dating then you should listen to them. When you are physically attracted to someone your brain is not turned on, so pay attention to warnings from your support group.

When you have finally had enough and decide to leave, be prepared for the responses you may get. If you believe that the abuser may become violent then make sure you are not alone with the abuser when you tell him or her. Violence is always a possibility, but they may try the opposite tactic-crying and pleading. Ever heard the expression, crocodile tears? Remember it when you have someone bawling and hanging onto you, begging for another chance. Do not give in. They do not mean it and will get even with you or your children for trying to take control. No matter what the source of their behavior is, whether the abuser was beaten as a child or is an alcoholic, it is not your problem and you did not cause his or her abusive behavior. Tell your family or close friends if you are in a bad situation. Forget the humiliation and embarrassment of making a bad choice, everyone does something they wish they had not. Abusers count on you not having anyone to help you, so do not isolate yourself. I'll say it again. Do not isolate yourself from people that care about you just because they may say things about your partner that you do not like. If most of the people you know do not like your partner, then you need to wake up and smell the proverbial coffee or in this case, feces.

Don't be afraid to call the police if you or your children are being abused . The abuser will be arrested and if he or she is the type to make bail and come right back and cause more pain, then don't be there when they get out. Call a lawyer or if you don't have money call legal aid. You can call a women's shelter in your area for advise. For a heterosexual man that is being abused the situation is harder as society has not kept up with the times. Women are becoming more aggressive and there are men in similar situations as abused women. What a man could do is call a local church in his area that ministers to the gay community, as most have groups for abused men, and explain his situation. The gay community is very open and responsive to a wide range of people and their problems. It might be one solution for a man that does not want to tell his family or friends he is being abused by his female partner. People are people. What makes a woman abuse other people is not that different from her male counterpart and the same goes for victims.

What does domestic violence have to do with child abuse? Everything. People that remain in abusive households with men or women that abuse children are most often either physically or mentally abused themselves. They believe that there is no life without the abuser, that they could not make it on their own. Fear of being alone or being hunted down by the abuser is a big deterrent to leaving, but one that must be overcome. Those that will not leave bad environments are now called enablers

My mother would have been very hurt to be called an enabler. Joyce thought that she could keep Al from abusing us and spare us the trials of poverty and a broken home. Mom truly meant well, but there is nothing one can do to stop a pedophile or those that like to use children as punching bags. Those that like to rape or beat children will find a way to do it no matter who is watching them. The desire that pedophiles possess to rape children is amazing. When I worked at a maximum security prison there was a visitation room that would hold around a hundred visitors, inmates and officers. Even in that environment, sex offenders found a way to molest their children-it was that important to them and who knows how many times they diddled their kids before they were caught doing it?

The whole idea behind the "enabler" concept is that abusers cannot harm other people without being allowed to do so. While it makes sense, it also is very black and white and too simple. It assumes that if people tell and ask for help that they will get it. In our case there were many enablers-the cops, shrinks, social workers, ministers, probation officers and the U.S. Army. There have been many cases of known abuse situations where no action is taken to stop the abuse and society is the enabler

For those that find themselves married to or living with a pedophile there is only one thing you can do-get the hell out of that relationship.

There is no cure for pedophilia and they are masters at raping children under your nose. No amount of therapy will stop them, no amount of prison time. Pedophiles stop raping children when they are rotting in the ground and not before. They deserve no pity, even those that claim they do it because they were molested as kids. Anyone that has suffered from the acts of a pedophile knows the pain and misery it causes and if they choose to turn around and do it to someone else, they are no better.

Telling people about sexual abuse is not easy and I won't tell anyone that it is. I would rather have just had an alcoholic father or one who ran off with some bimbo, but there is something about rape that is very dark and destructive. Our forefathers were smarter than we are today as murder, rape and kidnaping used to get you the rope. They did not feel that such people could be rehabilitated and they were not about to pay for their keep if they could not contribute to society. I can understand why you might want or need to kill someone or steal something, but never could there be a good explanation for raping a child or anyone else for that matter. Rape is a completely negative act with negative consequences and those that chose to do it should be shown no mercy.

I have a web site titled, "Silence is a Pedophile's Lethal Weapon." Silence is the most potent of any abuser's weapon's cache, next to threats. If you are afraid to call the police or too apprehensive about talking to family , then find someone you can talk too. If necessary go to the Women's Studies section of nearby university and talk to a professor there as she would know who could help you. There are people who will be outraged by what you tell them and they should be-you owe no loyalty to an abuser. No one has the right to use you and your children as a punching bag either physically or emotionally. The law cannot help you if you are not willing to go the full mile. The abuser needs to do prison time and your sympathy is wasted on that person.

The best advice I can give is, do not take any kind of abuse from any-one. No second chances. If you are punched in the face for some remark you made, move out or throw that person out. Ignore the pleas and prom-ises of doing better or getting help. You are not a proving ground. Your life is precious and you only get one, so do not allow someone with serious problems to ruin that one lifetime. You are not the Annie Sullivan of abusers or Lassie to the rescue of some poor sap drowning in his own self hatred. Get out of bad relationships and never rush to move in with some-one you barely know

If you are raising children as a single parent, the welfare of your chil-dren come first. Do not allow people to call your children names, hit them or sexually abuse them. There are actually women out there who side with the abuser against a teenage daughter for, "giving the guy the come on." Never put some guy you are dating or shacking up with over your chil-dren. It will come back to haunt you and may cause you to lose custody of your children.

You must remember that you are a human being that does not deserve to be tormented day in and day out. If your partner has more bad than good to say about you, there is a problem. There are many worst things than being single. Relationships are suppose to benefit both parties and they work best when both parties have good mental health. Don't enter into a relationship thinking it will solve some great emptiness within you. If you are not happy with yourself and have little self respect, then you are setting yourself up for abuse.

Ready for church

Ready for church. Mom wrote on the back, " The sweetest kids in the world."

Chapter Three

Good Touch, Bad Touch?

Let's get down to brass tacks. Child sexual abuse is rape and until the law recognizes that fact pedophiles will continue to get their wrists slapped. It is a sexual act and terms such as fondling, molesting, indecent liberties and incest are just nicely labels society uses to avoid the real issue. People are also fond of saying that rape is not about sex. Who ever said that has never been raped. A society that doesn't mind showing graphic sex acts on television runs into shadows when talk of child rape is discussed. When a child is sexually abused what really occurs? Whatever two adults can do to together, a pedophile can inflict on a child. Which means oral sex and vaginal and anal penetration. Al liked to have his sons anally penetrate him, but fortunately I was left out of the penetration activity. Most pedophiles seem to have a preference for one sex or the other, however, they will take which ever is available. I believe that one reason society does not make a major effort to eliminate pedophiles is the terminology used to describe the actions. Fondling? Sounds like someone flipping around a Basset Hound's ears! Molesting is a nineteenth century term for a man sitting too close to a strange woman on a park bench. Indecent liberties? What the hell is that? Uncle Charlie took little Johnny to see The Graduate?

Don't have a clear picture of sexual abuse yet? Try imagining some scumbag running his tongue up your little girl's vagina. Do you call that "fondling"? We need to get the definition of rape changed to include both sexes and no age limits. Rapist is a label no one wants placed on them, especially guys like Al who convince themselves that children look forward to their horror sessions. Want to see a chickenhawk bristle up? Call him a rapist.

I can tell you that the terms, good touch, bad touch, mean little to children in abusive situations. They will not recognize sexual behavior from such general terminology and you must remember that pedophiles know children very well. Abusers can paint the situation so pretty that it is sometimes years later that children realize what was done to them. Of course, by that time the Statue of Limitations will rescue the majority of child rapists from prosecution. Children are the perfect victims. They have limited language capabilities, are naive, do not remember exact dates and times and are easily manipulated or threatened. Children are often lousy witness and there are many prosecutors who will not even try to convict if there is no evidence other than the child's word. There are many sexual acts a pedophile can do to a child that will not leave physical evidence and a child can be convinced that the predator is doing the child favor. Pedophiles are often people you would never suspect. They are everywhere in every occupation. They are good at staining honorable positions such as the Catholic priesthood and boy scout leaders. Chickenhawks have managed to get the spot light off of them and onto gay men as is demonstrated in the policy of the Boy Scouts of America. Sorry, but the majority of pedophiles are heterosexual men. When a child comes in contact with a non-relative abuser, it will probably be someone whom the child has been taught to respect and obey. If this person asks the child to do something, then it cannot be a "bad touch." Pedophiles like to buy gifts and give money to further win the child over. The abuser that hurts your child will not fit the image a child might have as a "bad" person.

So what can a parent do? First, don't give your children cute names for their private areas. Like it or not, children of the new millennium are more sophisticated than generations past. Use the proper names for sexual anatomy; penis. vagina and breasts. Tell them no one other than a doctor or nurse should be touching their sexual parts and only then if in a hospital or doctor's office. Don't ask the question, "Has anyone hurt you?", because that may not ring any bells either. Sexual acts can feel good no matter who is doing it, so the child may not understand that this act was "hurting" them.

Explain to children that there are such people as pedophiles who like to have sex with children. A child should be taught to be alarmed by an adult who exposes his or her sexual organs to the child and to tell someone immediately. They should be told to run and never keep the secret, especially if the child cannot get away from the abuser. Many pedophiles would take off if a child screamed or said no to requests for oral sex and other activities, but remember that child sexual abuse is rape. There are situations when a child would have to carefully consider how much to resist. Sadistic pedophiles would kill a child if necessary to avoid detection.

Pay attention if a child suddenly does not want to do a favorite activity or go with someone whose company they previously enjoyed. It may not mean sexual abuse, but could indicate some other type of problem. Behavior often speaks louder than words. An angry personality in a normally happy child should raise red flags as well as getting into fights and a fascination with fire. A sudden drop of grades in school or a distinct lack of respect for authority should also trigger alarm in a parent. The child may have been threatened if he told about being sexually abused and will not say anything, but they are telling you something in their behavior.

Not all sexually abused children will display poor grades or destructive behavior. I never did, but I had music, art and writing to absorb my pain. Children that don't cause society any trouble tend not to be noticed and give some the impression that sexual abuse isn't that bad if a child can sail through it with little noticeable damage. A large percentage of violent felon's report being sexually abused as children, so while some children manage to cope with the abuse, many more do not. If society cares about nothing else, it should care about the millions of dollars pedophiles cause the taxpayers.

If a child does tell you they are being abused, it may be someone who will shock you. Never call the child a liar or trivialize the experience. Ask the child what happen and where then call the police. You have an obligation to report abuse of a child and it does not matter who did the abusing. It may turn out that the child misinterpreted the adult's actions, but it needs to be investigated if it caused the child anguish. There are many people being convicted of child abuse that are not guilty, but accusations of abuse still need to be investigated before being dismissed. Sexual abuse is a hot potato that often burns the innocent without harming the abuser, which aids in the lack of convictions for child abusers.

Chapter Four

The Incest Exception Laws

Incest is the Holy Grail of pedophiles. Hide in plain site. They disguise themselves as members of a respectable All American Family and no one suspects a thing. Marry and produce your own victims and the law will look the other way. If they are lucky, their victims will produce grand-victims and the story goes on and on and on. What a glorious day it must have been for the first chickenhawk to figure that one out! The chances of being charged and convicted are much greater with someone else's children, so why bother? The incest laws were intended to prevent close relatives from marrying and reproducing children with birth defects. They were never intended to aid pedophiles in their efforts to evade prison, but aid them they do. My brother, Mark, always said that the laws favor pedophiles because they are making the laws. Makes you wonder, doesn't it? Who decided that being raped by your father was much less traumatic that by a stranger? No one who has ever experienced it I can assure you. There is a great reluctance to prosecute cases of incest and the offender usually gets probation when the law bothers to do anything at all. The incest exception laws stemmed from the days when girls where married off at twelve years old and often to a relative. Marriage is among one of the situations excluded in the laws regarding abuse. So, if one wished to marry a twelve year old they would not be committing a crime when having sex with that child. Regardless of the original intention of the Incest Exception laws, all they do now is guarantee that pedophiles can have a free-for-all with blood relatives. They are antiquated laws that need to be done away with, but congress doesn't see it that way. Congress would like to keep rewarding those that are smart enough to breed their own victims and want everyone to shut up about it. I seriously wonder about the character of any politician that did not support the Care Act of 1999.

The Care Act of 1999 challenged the incest exception laws and was sponsored by Representative Bob Ney. The act directly targeted the luke warm punishments given to those that restrict their sexual abuse to blood relatives, but it died due to lack of interest. Is there any wonder why sexual abuse goes on from on from one generation to another? It really seems that no one cares if your daddy makes you suck his penis as along as he stays off the welfare rolls. Ney plans to keep reintroducing the bill until it passes and he is to be commended for this dedication as are the forty co-sponsors of the bill. The Care Act has a web page that is worth visiting and we should do all we can to make sure it one day passes.
Http://www.careact.org

The Forty Co-Sponsors of the Care Act

Name	State/District	Contact Information
Robert W. Ney	OH 18	http://www.house.gov/ney
Michael G. Oxley	OH 4	http://www.house.gov/oxley
Earl F. Hilliard	AL 7	http://www.house.gove/hilliard
Curt Weldon	PA 7	http://www.house.gov/curtweldon
Bob Barr	GA 7	http://www.house.gov/barr
Michael K. Simpson	ID 7	http://www.house.gov/simpson
Robert A. Underwood	Guam	http://www.house.gov/underwood
James A. Barcia	MI 5	http://www.house.gov/barcia
Lynn N. Rivers	MI 13	http://www.house.gov/rivers
Chris Smith	NJ 14	http://www.house.gov/chrissmith
Johnny Isakson	GA 6	http://www.house.gov/isakson
Ken Lucas	KY 4	http://www.house.gov/kenlucas
Zach Wamp	TN 3	http://www.house.gov/wamp
George Nethercutt Jr.	WA 5	http://www.house.gov/nethercutt
Pat Danner	MO 6	http://www.house.gov/danner
Joseph Pitts	PA 16	http://www.house.gov/pitts
Joe Baca	CA 42	http://www.house.gov/baca
Gary Miller	CA 41	http://www.house.gov/garymiller
Donna Christian-Christensen U.S. Virgin Isl.		http://www.house.gov/christian-christensen
Dan Burton	IN 6	http://www.house.gov/burton
Steve Largent	OK 1	http://www.house.gov/largent

Merrill Cook UT 2		http://www.house.gov/cook
James Traficant Jr. OH 17		http://www.house.gov/traficant
Gene Taylor MS 5		http://www.house.gov/genetaylor
Tom Delay TX 22		http://tomdelay.house.gov
Karen Thurman FL 5		http://www.house.gov/thurman
Steve Chabot OH 1		http://www.house.gov/chabot
Mark Souder IN 4		http://www.house.gov/souder
Mike McIntyre NC 7		http://www.house.gov/mcintyre
Wayne Gilchrest MD 1		http://www.house.gov/gilchrest
Christopher Shays CT 4		http://www.house.gov/shays

Name	State/District	Contact Information
Ken Calvert	CA 43	http://www.house.gov/calvert
Nick Rahall	WV 3	http://www.house.gov/rahall
Patsy T. Mink	HI 2	http://www.house.gov/mink
Vernon Ehlers	MI 3	http://www.house.gov/ehlers
Joseph Hoeffel	PA 13	http://www.house.gov/hoeffel
Tom Latham	IA 5	http://www.house.gov/latham
Tom Bliley	VA 7	http://www.house.gov/bliley
Peter DeFazio	OR 4	http://www.house.gov/defazio

I am very disappointed to note that not one name from Kansas is on that list. Kansas is a state that thumps the Bible loudly and parades family values like a float in a Thanksgiving Day parade, yet not one of our representatives backed this bill. Unless they think incest is a family value, I cannot imagine why this bill was not backed one hundred percent. It would be nice if Kansas politicians could be known for something besides Viagra, but then maybe that sends a message of its own? The Kansas Attorney General deserves to be mentioned for her efforts to keep child predators off the streets. Carla Stovall wanted to make sure that when a pedophile served his prison time, he had to then go to a psychiatric facility for treatment. Many other states contacted Stovall for information on how they too could set up such program. Sex offenders will do it again, but there are those that care only for the rights of these pieces of human waste and fight against those trying to protect society. Stovall is one of very few politicians that I hold in high regard and we need more that are unafraid to say what needs to be said.

The usual response is that we already have laws in place and do not need anymore. If they are not enforced then they may as well not exist. The incest exception laws need to be eliminated. It is never okay to rape your children, nieces, nephews, cousins or step children. Rape is rape and is it not better if you only sexually abuse your own relatives. Pedophiles think there is a difference too. The ones that only do strangers kids think they are superior to those that only rape their own kids and visa versa. Both groups were spawned in Hell and both rank equally on the scum meter. Let's get the laws changed!

Chapter Five

Children in a Dark, Scary Place Called Incest

Theoretically, your home is your safe haven from the world. Home should bring warm thoughts and a strong desire to be there, but the child that is being sexually abused by a family member is trapped in a strange place. The situation is many times worst for families that move around with jobs in the military or ministry or what ever occupation keeps them on the road. Such families tend to be close knit because they are strangers and outsiders everywhere they go. It is important that they have each other and that home truly is a sanctuary. It is also the ideal situation for the predator.

Something about sexual abuse eats a child from the inside out. You never entirely get over it and some kill themselves long before adulthood. I took an overdose of pills in high school and was only saved because my parents returned home to get my mother's purse. I felt like I was forty years old and could not bear the idea that I could have another fifty years of living to endure. It was an overwhelming thought that lay on me like a slab of cement and nothing that I was interested in doing. I was truly wore out from life. My only periods of happiness existed when my father was gone and even then his essence hovered over head like a death's head moth waiting to land on me. Sexually abused children are different from other children and somehow "normal" children know it. They circle the abused child like a pack of wolves that cannot decide whether to let the new wolf join the pack or eat it for dinner. If I had been a beautiful child or had an outgoing personality, it may have helped, but I hated myself. I would rather have stood on a bed of burning coals than look at myself in a mirror and if it appeared that I might have some self respect, Al would fix that for me. He ran his sisters down constantly and used them to make me feel bad. I was often compared to my Aunt Everett and it was meant as an insult. Now I know that my father's sisters grew up watching their mother be beaten to the floor by their minister father and had problems of their own. It is all very clear now that Al dug a moat around us so that no one could really get that close. Fortunately, my aunt and grandmother had a pontoon boat that could occasionally reach our island, even if they never got past the beach. I only made it because I knew there was another world out there that did not include pornography and lewd acts. When I should have been an innocent child, I knew more about sex than some people ever do.

To make matters worst, I was a major tomboy. Al had wanted a boy as his first child and if not, then a prissy girl. Well, I was not either. I hated everything that girls were supposed to like and wanted nothing to do with traditional womanhood. My time was spent playing army and climbing trees and I could not possibly have hated dresses more than I did. In 1967 Al made me wear jeans that were pastel colors, then would blister my butt for getting dirty. He would get mad when I wanted trucks instead of dolls. While Mom would be proud of my music and art, Al would tell me those talents were worth nothing. Only those good at math were successful and

I barely passed it. Later I found out that I have a learning disability that causes me to reverse numbers, but Al (and several teachers)told me that I was just stupid. Mark had a similar experience with dyslexia.

Since I could have very little in life the way I wanted it, I took control where I could. There were times that I simply did not wake up and wet the bed and other times when I did it on purpose. It did not take long to learn that the son-of-a-bitch would turn around and leave at the smell of urine. I also liked to perform commando raids on the kitchen where I would climb up on the cupboards and procure a few Scooter Pies for my stock pile. I didn't strangle cats like Mark did, but I enjoyed placing a firecracker in a toad's mouth and watching the sucker completely flip over. Al didn't show me the strangle a cat while you masturbate trick. What is that? Autoeroticism by proxy?

When we lived at Independence Hill, Virginia, Mark and me spent a great deal of time playing in the woods. Some kids were afraid of perverts that might sneak up on them, but when you live with the chief asshole of the bunch, there isn't much to fear in the forest. We would pray that Al would have a wreck on the way home and die, but that never happened. I began to have a real problem with God, Who seemed to be on the side of the wicked and cruel. At least I had plenty of hobbies and interests to bury myself in, but Mark did not. Unfortunately for Mark his main passion was firearms, which Al would never allow in the house. He had this idea that Mark would kill him if given the means and he was correct. The only reason that Mark did not kill our father was Mom begged Mark not to throw his young life away, so he promised not to kill Al.

I shall never understand those that live only to degrade and torment other people. Al made sure that even meal times were a misery. To this day I cannot tolerate screaming, loud cussing or slamming things around as the first decade of my life was filled with it. There are times when certain sounds and smells bring everything rushing back to me like a tidal wave of manure. One of the things both me and Mark hated about being close to Al was his stale cigarette and coffee breath. His lips were like two slugs struggling to attach themselves to your face. The smell of his penis is something that will not elude me either. If I could do it all again I would have bitten the damned thing off-how could he have explained that one? As a child I was jealous of Mark for being born a boy. He could dress the way I wanted to and do the things that I wanted to do, but being a girl had one advantage. If I had been a boy, I would have had to stick my little organ into Al's gaping anus and for that lack of experience I am grateful. Mark was not that lucky. Mark really had no luck at all. I often wonder what would have happened if he had not had diabetes and could have been the Green Beret he longed to be. Life could have been very different for Mark Chadwick if he had just caught one little break, but Mark spent most of his short life paying for Al's sadistic acts. When I would watch my sobbing mother sit with her hand on the phone and never dial it, I would wonder what Al did to her in private. She would tell me while weeping that she wanted to call her mother and sister for help, but how could she tell them what her husband had done? It was so awful and shameful that one could hardly speak the words. Mom was also terrified that she would lose custody of us and never get us back. I know that fear had been ground into her by Allan the Bad as he did it to me. I am still not so sure that Al could not have arranged for Mom to be charged while he walked. He always said that if we told he would blame it on Mom and after she died he did just that.

After we found the pictures of JonBenet Ramsey in Al's drawer, me and my sister put an ad in the local shopper's guide indicating that a certain child molester whose wife had died and who lived next door to a cop, should move out of town. Well, it did not take long for the police to figure out who the ad referred to and they searched Al's house for two hours looking for child porn. They should have known that when he gave consent for a search that Al had already removed what he had in the house. Al left a message on my answering machine saying the cops had been there and to call him about it. He sounded more stressed that I had ever heard him. A short time later he left another message that the cops wanted to talk to me. He had that cocky voice that he used when he was going to screw over his wife or children. Al assumed that I put the ad in the paper as his other children all adored him and it had to have been his wicked oldest daughter who would want daddy in jail.

When I called the chief of detectives he told me that my dad was there and would I come down and talk with them? I said sure and my sister would too , but not with Al in the room. It wasn't hard to figure out Al's game plan. He would degrade me in front of the cops then skip happily out the door, just like always. The detective told us that Al blamed the sexual abuse on Mom and that is was all her idea. Of course, he also boo hooed about his pathetic childhood and told the police how his father used to beat his mother to the floor. The only story we ever heard was how his mother whacked his father on the head with a broom at the dinner table. I said, " Well, that's a new version to us." In all my life I've never heard a mean word said about Joyce Erwin Chadwick, except what filth came from Allan Chadwick

There was a playhouse at Mom's that she had planned to fix up for the grandchildren, but after eighteen months of asking Al to help her it was still not done. Mom was diagnosed with cancer and began chemotherapy in March 1997. She wasn't able to work on the little house, but Al immediately started work on it the minute Mom was dead. We all know why he wanted to attract children. The man who did no physical activity all of a sudden went for walks past the grade school and volunteered to do fire checks at the daycare where my mother had worked. He knew that my mother would have been very unhappy to see him anywhere near that daycare. She did not allow him to come there.

Al's cruelty to my mother her last few months of life will haunt me forever. When she told Al that she was not going to live he simply said, "Well, whatever will be will be", then took his fried chicken into the house to eat it. Never did he ever offer to make a meal for her and ignored her deteriorating health. He expected her to still care for his raggedly, worthless ass when the very life was draining out of her. A few hours after she died on October 25, 1997, Al was after me and my sister to get Mom's stuff out of the house. Right before she took her last breath he was only concerned with where he was going to eat breakfast. He was happy that Mom was going to die because he truly believed that he would be allowed to molest his grandchildren and those in the neighborhood. The old hag that was ruining his good times was finally out of the way.

On her death bed my mother asked Al what happened to her last pay check from the daycare. He patted his wallet and said it was in there. Mom wanted it back so that my aunt could take her shopping for Christmas presents as Mom knew she was not going to be on earth by that time. Al refused to give it to her. He also stole the money she wanted us to have from her life insurance policy. F ortunately for Al, Mom died before I could help her write a new will. An existing will was in the house, but Al refused to give it to her. She had a feeling that he could not be trusted to carry out her wishes and he certainly did not. One of my mother's last wishes was for my adopted handicapped daughter to be buried near her and Mom made Al buy eight plots to make sure it happened. It will not happen as Al always referred to Anita as a double negative that contributes nothing to society; sort of sounds like he was describing himself

I know that in the last few days of my mother's life she realized that she meant nothing at all to the husband whom she had endured untold suffering. She kept pushing him away whenever he tried to get near her and I try not to think of what terrible things he probably said to her. In the end

Mom knew that he only married her to produce victims. It is a tragedy that she ever met that soul sucker. Mom was very nice looking and liked by everyone who met her. He certainly did not deserve her or the children they had together. We cannot change the past, but my mother's story can be used to help other young mother's out there who find themselves in this dreary realm of existence.

Al, and those like him, are festering pus bags that walk this earth solely to spread evil and pain. Society needs to wake up and start giving a damn about those that prey on the children they produce. One good thing about modern society is that child abuse, sexual abuse and domestic violence are now openly discussed. This was not so when we were children. If a man abused his wife and kids in the 1960s, then they must have done something to make him do it. The poor man works all day and is entitled to knock his old lady around and diddle the kids because God made him the head of the household. The Mormon's believe that a woman only enters heaven through the priesthood of her husband. If that is the case, I won't be going at all and Mom will only go if Al thinks she deserves it. I have nothing clean to say about this sort of thinking and believe it is the bane of humanity. No one should rule without question. A child trapped in a house with a pedophile parent at least has a few options today. They can tell and may be taken from the home, but I doubt it. The abuser might be made to leave, but that is doubtful also as someone decided that making the pedophile leave the home causes children more anguish. What a load of crap! Having learned what I know about pedophiles the hard way and not from textbooks, I know this is not true. It might be true if the parent is innocent of any wrong doing. I could never imagine being unhappy with the removal of Al from our lives. I have not known anyone else who would have been upset to see their rapist father in handcuffs either.

If I had to relive the horror of my childhood I would hurt my father every chance that presented itself. Every time he tried to kiss me I would bite him. When he put my hand on his erect penis I would squeeze until his eyeballs popped out of his skull. If he leaned over me in my bed I would punch him in the throat. I would never go anywhere with him alone. I would scream and make a horses' rear end of myself by the car until the neighbors all stared at him. When he tried to make Mark and me participate in orgies we would have beaten him black and blue, but hindsight is a wonderful thing and I am not a helpless child anymore. But then, that's what makes children so attractive as victims. If I could turn back time I would tell my grandmother and aunt what was happening to us and that is my biggest regret. I wish that I had done what my mother could not as I felt no bond or loyalty to Al. It would have been the crowning glory of my childhood to see Al in prison clothes and a dishonorable discharge from the army. In a justice world that is exactly what would have happened.

Children being sexually abused at home need to tell and keep telling until someone does something about the situation. It takes an enormous amount of courage to describe the nasty acts a pedophile does to a child and to take the consequences of telling. No child wants their home torn apart or the non-offending parent to suffer, but neither can a child spent life dreading each day. The predator has made the home a non safe environment and a place of fear-which should be a violation of civil rights at the most basic level. Pedophiles do all they can to rob a child of liberty and happiness.

I would like to see an end to the laws protecting the Allan Boyce Chadwick's of the world. They know that they are worth more than their children and they know they won't do any jail time. Anyone that doubts the cockiness of modern pedophiles just needs to cruise the Internet. The legal term of incest is a free walk for child rapists. Rape is rape and is does not matter whom is doing it to whom or the age of the victim and offender. My father turned us all into prostitutes for a roof over our heads and food to eat and all society ever did to him was pat him on the back and tell him what a great guy is. Child abuse has to stop, especially sexual abuse.

Chapter Six

The Internet

The Internet is a wonderful invention. We can talk to people in Europe we would other wise not even know existed. Research is much easier and more thorough. Information and ideas can be traded and shared and new musicians and writers can now be heard when before the Internet they would never have had a chance. The world is open to both children and adults. We can correspond with people instantaneously anywhere without postage stamps and there is no turning back.

Unfortunately, child predators have discovered the Internet as well. They are just as good at preying on children in the virtual world as they are in the real one. Fathers that sexually abuse their children are taking pictures and sharing them on line with other chickenhawks who may be less fortunate in that they have no children to abuse. When I was working with the organization, Guardian Angels Watching Over Them(GAWOT), we found the most offensive pictures imaginable. One picture was of a five year old girl sucking on the penis of a dog and there is never any shortage of photos of children in sexual positions with adults or other children.

There was one picture of a two year old girl with her father's face between her legs and he looked so much like my father it was scary. Al never had the gonads to take pictures back then, but if he could have used the Internet it would have been a whole different story

How easy is it to find such pictures or meet pedophiles on the web? Very easy. One of the main areas to watch are the communities such as Yahoo groups and MSN communities. A parent needs to keep a close eye on what sites their children prefer on the Internet and check them out. Pedophiles are sneaky when baiting children and will join communities for young children as a child themselves. Those that like to sexually abuse children know more about what children like than their parents do. They know the latest toys, cartoons, comic books, movies, music, fashions and what toys are in Happy Meals. Predators can talk to your child in their language and know the latest slang words.

Adolescents think they know everything and cannot be fooled, but they are tricked by pedophiles daily. A ten year old girl could be positive that she is conversing with another ten year old girl when it is really a thirty year old man who has been telling her about his newest CD. GAWOT has members who teach children how easily they can be fooled by posing as children. When they get all the personal information they can from the child, they call that child at home. It is usually a big shock to the child when some adult calls and identifies themselves as the child's eleven year old Internet friend, but it is a lesson not forgotten. Parents who would like to find out how easy it is to put child porn on the web should go to one of the many communities such as MSN, Yahoo, Excite, etc and type in the keywords, boy lover, daddy's little girl or some similar phrase. Before doing that, however, set up a non-server based email under a phony name as most of these communities require you to join before allowing access. Among the many legitimate members in the group are the pedophiles and their dirty pictures. While groups such as GAWOT shut many of these sites down, the offenders just move on to other sites until they are caught. You will find that many pedophiles will place their pictures in profiles and some are bold enough to include their faces in sex acts with children. Most will cut out facial shots, but it is amazing the number who don't feel this is necessary. Pedophiles do not fear the law as it usually serves to benefit them. There are some sex offenders who make elaborate web sites proclaiming their "sexual preference for children". Congress has decided that outlawing virtual child porn is a violation of free speech. If our forefathers could see what sort of trash the constitution has been used to defend they would be sick. Pedophiles need to be exterminated, not encouraged. There are many web sites that offer support for victims of sexual abuse and most of them are legitimate, but be wary. Pedophiles like to cruise these groups for the vulnerable and emotionally damaged. Message boards with subjects like," I enjoyed being sexually abused as anyone else?", should send up a red flag as this is a ploy pedophiles use to have dialogue with victims. Pedophiles want to believe that children enjoy being raped and constantly seek endorsement for their actions. I have seen this type of trap on my own message board, "What Do You Think Should Be Done to Stop Child Molesters?" Sex offenders wander the web looking for the stories that victims tell about their sexual abuse so they can relive the pleasure they last felt when abusing a child. They filter out the pain in these sad tales and focus only on the sexual aspects. Know who your children are conversing with on the web. I actually had pedophiles email me after viewing my web pages and ask if I brought the abuse on myself or if it was really rape. It was a good thing for him that I did not know where he lived! The attitude is typical of child rapists. Pedophiles believe that they are a persecuted group whom society targets for no good reason. They try to convince each other that society brainwashes children to think sexual abuse is harmful. Children would like to perform sexual acts on adults if society didn't tell them not to enjoy it. The study by Rind only aids this philosophy when it suggests using the term, child-adult sex. My own father would wet his pants in excitement over this crowning endorsement of his actions. He always tried to convince us that Mom was against anything that was fun and if it were not for her, we could do sexual things with him even more often. I did not enjoy being made to have oral sex with him nor will I ever forgive him for it. No child likes being taught the details of sex by a parent and only pedophiles think that way.

In addition to scouting around victim support groups, pedophiles have their own support groups. They are not about ceasing their criminal activity, but are information exchanges. These groups have titles such as , The Boy Lover Support Group. Some members will whine about how society discriminates against them or how they can't stop lusting after children, but most share information about where to find the best child porn pictures on the web. The problem is world wide. Chickenhawks have a network that spans the globe from Texas to Latvia and every time one of their sites is shut down, they immediately set up shop elsewhere.

The Internet has made it very easy for perverts to obtain pictures and home movies containing sexual abuse and a favorite topic is incest. The battle against those that prey on children will never be won until the law stops defending them. Rape is not an example of free speech and it is not okay if child porn is converted to a cartoon. Animal rights groups do more to those that abuse dogs than the courts do to those who rape children.

Web Sites to Report Child Porn on the Internet

All links were working at the time of publication.

Guardian Angels Watching Over Them
http://www.gawot.org

The Judicial Police
http://www.gpj.be/uk/gpj-e-form.html

Report Child Porn and Predators
http://pedowatch.org

Child Abuse.com
http://www.childabuse.com

CyberArmy Striving for a Child Friendly Planet
http://www.antichildporn.org/cyberarmy.html

Predator Hunter Inc.
Http://www.predator-hunter.com

Stop Child Abuse
http://www.stop-abuse.de

Report Child Porn
http://ww.reportchildporn.com

The above groups are just a few working to rid the Internet of child predators.

Helpful Child Abuse Links

Child Sexual Abuse
http://www.cs.vtk.edu/~bartley/sacc/childabuse.html

Child Abuse Prevention Network
http://child.cornell.edu

Reynold's House A personal story

http://www.proteus.demon.co.uk/Reynolds.htm

Child Abuse Yellow Pages
http://idealist.com/cayp

Save Guarding Our Children-United Mothers
http://www.soc-um.org

Prevent Child Abuse America
http://www.preventchildabuse.org

Dale A. Koon's Child Abuse Prevention Page
http://members.iquest.net/~dkoons

Care Act of 1999
http://www.careact.org

Stop Child Porn On the Internet
http://www.thecpac.com/stop-it.html

Survivors of Incest Anonymous World Service Office
http://www.siqwso.org

Rape Abuse Incest National Network (RAINN)
http://www.rainn.org 1-800-799-SAFE(7233) 1-800-787-3224 (TDD)

V.O.I.C.E.S. In Action Victims of Incest Can Emerge Survivors
http://www.voices-action.org/index.html

Post-Incest Syndrom in Women and Men-The Incest Survivor After Effects Check List http://www.efn.org/~terra/incest.html

The Domestic Violence and Incest Resource Center (DUIRC)
http://home.vicnet.net.au/~duirc

Menweb Surviving and Living-Male Survivors and Child Sexual Abuse
http://www.vix.com/menmag/sexabupg.htm

Pandora's Box The Secrecy of Child Sexual Abuse
http://www.prevent-abuse-now.com

National Organization on Male Sexual Victimizaiton
http://www.malesurvivor.org

Survivor's Foundation
http://www.survivors-foundation.org

Abuse Recovery and Support for Survivors and Friends of Sexual Abuse
http://www.survivors-and-friends-org

No Longer a Victim Web Site for the Survivors of Sexual Abuse
http://www.justicefortheabused.org

Day of the Child
http://www.dayofthechild.org

Stop the Silence
http://www.geocities.com/solto/7130/silence.html

Twisted Roots of Evil Author Susan Kesegich
http://www.twist-of-fate.com

The Leadership Counsel for Mental Health, Justice and the Media
http://www.leadershipcounsel.org

National Clearinghouse on Child Abuse and Neglect Information
http://www.calib.com/nccanch

Sexual Assault Information Page
http://www.cs.utk.edu/~bartley/sahfoPage.html

Child Abuse: Statistics, Research and Resources Jim Hopper Ph.D
http://www.jimhopper.com/abstats

Center Against Sexual Abuse: Education, Prevention and Treatment
Indicators of Sexual Abuse http://www.syspac.com/~casa/indicato.htm

Breaking the Silence
http://www.breakingthesilence.com

Yes, International Child Abuse Network Break the Cycle
http://www.yesican.org

The Bridge Abuse Indicators
http://www.bridgecac.org/sexual4.html

American Humane Association
http://www.americanhumane.org

The Survivor's Page
http://www.stardate.bc.ca/survivors

Stop Domestic Violence Sgt Anne O'Dell 20 year veteran of the San Diego Police Department
http://www.stopdv.com/index2.htm

When Love Hurts A Guide for Girls on Love, Respect and Abuse in Relationships
http://home.vic.net.net.au/~girlsown

Men Against Domestic Violence Domestic Violence Recources
http://www.silcom.com/%7Epaladin/madv

Dr. Irene's Verbal Abuse Site
http://www.drirene.com/verbal.htm

Parent's for Megan's Law
http://www.parentsformeganslaw.com Excellent!

A Mother's Messge
http://chadwick59.homestead.com/joycechad.html

Silence is a Pedophile's Lethal Weapon
http://chadwick59.homestead.com/chickenhawks.html

Chapter Seven

A Brief Look at the Research Community

In 1997 Bruce Rind Ph. D of Temple University published a study called, *"A Meta-Analytic Examination of Assumed Properties of Child Sexual Abuse Using College Samples"* in the *Journal of Sex Research.* The work has ruffled a good many feathers and is commonly known as, The Rind Study. I am not sure just what Rind was trying to accomplish or how he hopes to help abused children, perhaps he has no such ambition. The basic theme is that unless sex is forced on a child or the child has close family ties with the abuser, childhood sex with can be a positive experience. In other words, if a thirty-five year old woman seduces a twelve year old boy, it is only a part of becoming a man. It is then child/adult sex, not abuse. This type of thinking is wrong and does an enormous disservice to those boys out there who did not find such an experience enlightening or enjoyable. Rind and his colleagues are in a minority in disputing that child sexual abuse is not all that bad nor are the effects long lasting. Such viewpoints are why sexual abuse is allowed to go on decade after decade. If a child can pull out of sexual abuse and go onto college, then society doesn't need to worry about it. In other words, as long as some children do not cause society any problems, society is not going to make the effort to stop pedophiles. Besides, child sexual abuse can be positive!

It is a great fear of mine that pedophiles are going to win out. They are equating their "movement" with the gay rights movement, women's suffrage and the Equal Rights Movement. What people need to realize is that the other causes all involve consenting adults who wish no harm to other people. Pedophiles want to have sex with your children. Sexual abuse at six years of age is not positive and you never really get over it, despite what sex offenders and some psychologists want the public to think. The reality is that anyone can eventually overcome a traumatic event, such as the Holocaust. It does not mean that it was okay for the Nazis to kill people because survivors of Auschwitz eventually became lawyers or opened doughnut shops!

In another article published in the *Journal of Sex Research*, Rind and Philip Tromovitch of the University of Pennsylvania conclude that it is premature to link maladjustment problems in later life to childhood sexual abuse. They indicate that if force is used or the abuser is closely related to the child, then the abuse can produce significant harm. Of course, this is the very point that pedophiles are trying to push; that they do not rape children. It does not take much for a child to believe that they have no choice but to obey an adult. So, if you can trade a candy bar for sex with a child ,then it is not forced. What is next on the agenda, arresting children for prostitution? Wouldn't my father love that one since he thinks we all secretly enjoyed it anyway and he did us a big favor by introducing us to the cruel world

McLean Hospital in Belmont, Massachusetts is a teaching hospital of Harvard Medical School and researchers there are doing impressive studies on the effects of child sexual and physical abuse on brain development. C.M. Anderson and a number of colleagues, including Martin Teicher, have published a paper on a study of sexually and verbally abused adults entitled, *Functional Asymmetry of the Temporal Lobes in Young Adults Verbally and Sexually Abused as Children Using fMRI*. In this study they found that in the abused adults there was a marked difference in the way the left and right hemispheres of the brain worked together. Sexual or verbal abuse can alter the temporal lobe development in children resulting in behavioral problems such as poor impulse control, limited stress tolerance, periodic aggression, inability to control anger and impaired memory.

The director of the Developmental Biopsychiatry Research Program, Martin Teicher, M.D. PhD, was awarded a million dollar research grant by the National Institute of Mental Health(NIMH) to continue on going research into adolescent brain development. The grant will allow Teicher and his colleagues, David Ennulat and Celeste LeBlanc to further study the causes of Attention deficit hyperactivity disorder(ADHD), Tourette's Syndrome and Schizophrenia.

Those who have grown up with abuse do not need to be told what sort of damages it can cause because they are forced to live with it, but it is encouraging that doctors realize that the effects of child abuse need to be studied. I only mention these two studies to show the ideas being explored today and how different the viewpoints can be. Teicher and his colleagues deserve all the positive feedback the research communities and the public can give them. As for Dr. Rind, he needs to do his research with those that live in maximum security prisons. There he will find the people who do not come through sexual abuse with flying colors but have earned their own wings as predators. Then there are the high school drop outs, those that marry abusers and those that cannot keep a job. We cannot leave out the abused children who end up walking the streets as prostitutes either.

Rind's attitude reflects those of society. As long as most abused children can go through the socially accepted motions, then sexual abuse didn't cause serious problems. Children that are sexually abused are crippled in some aspect forever. A good comparison might be an Olympic skier that breaks her leg in several places. She is able to ski for fun, but can never regain the speed and precision that she had before the trauma. Some people would think she should just be thankful that she wasn't killed, but fail to understand that she can never be the person she could have been if not for the injury. Sexual abuse too leaves an empty spot in the abused person's soul that is never quite healed.

If indeed sexual and verbal abuse cause the developmental problems that the McLean group believe they do, then what has society lost over the decades to abuse? Would society care more about sexual abuse if it knew that a cure for cancer could have been discovered a hundred years ago, but the boy who could have cured the disease was beaten and raped by his father and his brain never developed correctly? I believe that there are many survivors of sexual abuse who will never realize their full potential and the world has lost a great deal to predators. While I went to college, I did not become the doctor that I planned to be in high school because math causes my brain to short circuit. It is no coincidence that my brother, Mark, also had a learning disability. I wonder how different life could have turned out if I could have gone to medical school. Would my mother still be alive and would Mark's diabetes have been better controlled and he would also be alive now? I will never know because the law or social services never did anything to our father except make sure that he could continue the abuse of his children.

Sexual abuse does cause serious harm to children and Rind's work is suspicious in its motivations. Bruce Rind's background is in marketing research and his dissertation was entitled, *A Model for What Makes a Message Persuasive*. Rind did no original work on his study of sexually abused college students, but rather did an overview of studies done by other researchers. Supposedly forty-two percent of males claimed that their sexual abuse was a positive experience, while only eleven percent of females made the same statement. Rind's motivations for finding research to down play the negative effects of sexual abuse were made very clear when I found a Dutch publication entitled, *Paidika: The Journal of Pediophilia*. The mission of the journal is to show that pedophilia has always been and will remain a legitimate part of the whole human experience. It is a scholarly journal that promotes pedophilia and its only purpose is to gain acceptance for those that like to rape children. Of course, their point is that children are just as into sex with pedophiles as pedophiles are into sex with children. There is no rape and chickenhawks are just one more oppressed minority. It is obvious why Bruce Rind wants us all to think that sexual abuse of children is positive. The Rind Study is nothing but a marketing ploy to sell pedophilia to the masses.

There is also evidence that suggests that women who suffer childhood trauma early in life develop abnormal brain patterns that remain long after the abuse. Women who suffer child abuse can develop a severe over sensitivity to mild stress in adult life due to sharper hormonal and physical responses. Society cannot afford to coddle rapists any longer.

Chapter Eight

So The Child Has Told, So What Now?

The Parent

If you are the partner of the abuser do not rely on the police or social workers to solve your problem. Social Services is a funny creature that is outraged by a certain act one minute and could not care less an hour later. In the ideal situation, the abuser will be arrested and the courts will restrict the abuser's contact with the child, but do not count on it. The philosophy of the day is rehabilitation for everyone, including sex offenders, and the abuser may not be forced to leave the home. If the pedophile is told to leave the home, it will only be with the idea that the offender will one day return. In all likelihood family counseling will be ordered with the notion of repairing the family. Bullshit! The offender is broken, not the entire family, but you will all be made to feel as though you contributed to his/her illness. The cold reality is that pedophiles like to have sex with children and believe that they have the right to do so whether society likes it or not. Do not waste your time or expose your children to the offender any longer than necessary or as ordered by the court. Find a divorce lawyer and seek full custody of the children. There is no cure for pedophilia and nothing you do for the offender will make any difference. Your children will never be safe again from the abuser or at least not until they reach an age when they are no longer sexually attractive to the offender.

Pedophiles, like most abusers, will try all sorts of tricks to pull sympathy for them out of your rage. Don't be surprised at major bouts of crying or using your marriage vows to solicit guilt. For better or worst, you promised! Remember this little fact when reminded of the sanctity of marriage-the offender committed adultery against you with your own children. You owe nothing to the piece of manure that diddled your kids. Pedophiles are criminals and like all criminals they are masters of manipulation and care nothing for the well being of others. I'm not saying that turning your back on a partner will be easy, but you owe it to your children and yourself.

The relationship is over as you can never trust that person again. You cannot control every move of a pedophile and if they wish to molest children, they will and you cannot watch them twenty-four hours a day, seven days a week. No amount of therapy will ever change that fact. It is not possible to guard a pedophile constantly nor is it your lot in life. Get the abuser out of the house and do not allow unsupervised visits with your children. I realize this is harsh advise, but it is the only honest advise I can give. My mother, and many like her, have spent their entire lives trying to help those that cannot be helped. Pedophiles marry for two reasons-to produce victims and for appearances. Don't waste your time on a pedophile or risk the health of your children. They do not change and they do not want to change.

Once your child has told you of sexual abuse by a family member or someone outside the immediate family, then gather your support group. Do not try to face the coming dilemma alone. Do not expect anyone to show much compassion for the abuser and regardless of whatever he/she may have suffered as a child, they do not deserve sympathy for the sexual abuse of a child. There are people who will help you, but you must remember that you owe no loyalty to a child abusing partner and allow the help to be given. I hated therapy sessions as they always seemed to turn things around on us. Al was never the bad guy and no one ever suggested that he be punished or move out of the house even when there were small children to worry about. The audacity and pompous attitudes displayed by pedophiles are the result of society constantly looking the other way, especially if the abuser is a family member. Pedophiles do not fear the law because there is no reason for them to fear it.

Divorce and prosecution are the only weapons to use against a child sexual abuser and you must have the courage to make them happen. Anyone can marry or be involved with the wrong person, don't let embarrassment stop you from telling family and friends what is happening and that you need help. If you live far from family or close friends, then put the kids in the car and take off while the abuser is at work. You need back up in case the abuser strikes out physically, tries to blackmail you or threatens to harm the children or some other family member. Do not under estimate the power of emotional manipulation either. If you are not careful, the abuser will convince you to do nothing while they seek counseling for their problem. While they waste over a hundred dollars an hour whining to a shrink, they will prey on the kids. There are enough domestic abuse organizations in existence today that arranging for help is possible. No one needs to suffer in isolation anymore, but you have to make the first move which is the decision to play hardball with the abuser. Compassion is a wonderful human virtue providing it is not wasted on the wrong people. Never side with the abuser or make excuses for their actions. Save your children before the sexual abuse can damage them any further. You will have to work with the police, prosecutor and social services and it will probably be the hardest thing you will ever to in your life, but do it you must.

The Child

Sexual abuse is wrong no matter what sort of presents the adult may give you. No adult has the right to make you touch their penis or vagina and they should not touch yours. The adult might tell you that it is a secret, that you have a special relationship that other people would not understand. They tell you things like that because they know doing sexual acts with a child are wrong and they don't want to go to jail. The person abusing you may be your own parent, another relative or someone important in the community, but you must tell someone and get it stopped.

There is the possibility that even when you do tell, nothing will change and there are many reasons that could happen.

1. You may not be believed. Then tell someone else.

2. Your mother or father may be too afraid of the abuser to help you.

3. There may not be enough evidence to arrest or charge the abuser. Children often cannot Recall dates and times and the case may not make it to court.

4. You are believed, but for some reason the abuser is left in the home with you.

Regardless of the reason you are left to deal with an abusive adult, you must learn to survive the ordeal. You are not completely helpless, even if you are a small child

1. Try to avoid being alone with the person who abuses you. Don't let them close your bedroom door and if they do, then leave.

2. Don't sit on the abuser's lap

3. If he or she tries to put a hand down your pants or up your dress, slap their hand and say no. Get away from them.

4. If your abuser likes to come into your bedroom at night, wet the bed. You may get into trouble for doing it, but it is better than letting the abuser do bad things to you. 5. Do not worry about keeping peace in the family. If you are being abused it needs to be stopped and immediately.

6. When sex is forced on a person it is called rape. You do not have to have sex with adults no matter what they say or what they promise. You do not have to play fair. Sexual abuse is a crime and you should stop them from hurting you if you can.

7. Even though the behavior of the abuser may not cause physical pain it will make you feel strange and uncomfortable. It will feel wrong.

8. The abuser will try to convince you that what they do to you is okay, but it is not. 9. Abusers will try to turn you against your other parent, grandparents or friends. They will say that you are guilty too. Do not believe them.

10. Abusers will pretend that the two of you are pals or you are their favorite child and the sex acts they make you perform are special secrets just between the two of you. Sex with a child is a crime and it does not make you a special pal of the abuser, just a victim. 11. Sex with an adult is wrong even if they give you money or gifts. It is still rape. You do not have to trade sex for your Christmas or birthday presents either

Living with a child molester is the worst situation a child could endure, especially if the abuser is mean. If you tell people that you are being sexually abused and nothing is done to help you, then you as a child must fight back. The abuser plays dirty and if you feel that you cannot live one more day in misery, then strike back. Pedophiles pick on children because they are smaller and weaker so a child must wait until the abuser is weak. When is he the weakest? When his penis is hard and he is breathing heavy. If he makes you put your mouth on his penis, then bite it as hard as you can and run. He will be in enough pain that a child should be able to reach a phone or get outside to a neighbor's house. Make as much noise as possible, scream if you can. Bust every window in the house until you get someone to help you. There are many terrible things a pedophile can do to a child, including penetration of your vagina or rectum. Once again, get the abuser when he is the most occupied. Nothing hurts a man worst than hitting, kicking or scratching his erect penis. Remember that this advise is to be used when all else has failed and you are desperate. There is always the possibility that the abuser will turn violent, but chances are that you have been physically abused before and can endure one more punch. You must provide proof of sexual abuse when you have been either ignored in the past or no charges were brought against the abuser. If you bite off the man's penis, there is no explanation he can provide that would satisfy the police. There is no reason on earth that an adult's sexual organ should in the mouth of a child. None

I am aware that there are those that will disapprove of this book and its implications, but unless you have been at the mercy of a heartless, child-raping maggot, you cannot judge me. In a world that continues to fight for the rights of sex offenders, victims have to find their own way and their own solutions. Children that are being sexually abused by a family member are in the worst situation and their chances of being helped are far less than if a stranger abused them. The first decade of my life was spent having every moment of life tainted by a devil who had no fear of the law. My father turned every aspect of childhood into something vile and dark and as far as I am concerned there is no forgiveness for it. Those that forgive child abusers are guaranteeing that it will happen again and again-forgiveness for sex offences should be a crime. Rape eats a person from the inside out and there is no undoing it.

No child should have to endure a pedophile, especially if the abuser is a parent. The old saying that prevention is worth a pound of cure hits the nail on the head. Domestic abuse can be avoided altogether if people, particularly women, are taught self respect. If you have no feeling of self worth, you are only half a person and will tolerate whatever some thug wants to pass out. When you have no respect for your self, you cannot care for anyone else and will be too afraid to confront an abuser.

Allan and Joyce Erwin on----

Allan Chadwick and Joyce Erwin on their wedding day March 16, 1958. The happiness and hope of a new life are obvious on my mother's face. Fate is a cruel master indeed.

No Living in Crying

Lyrics and music by D.A. Chadwick 1999

There was a self man, who never would take a stand
and he always wore a frown
just to bring everybody down

He stayed away from the light
and everything that's right
hey, he should have done what he should
and stayed away from the good
But there ain't no habit like lying, there ain't no habit like lying

He met a woman from the light
Oh that lady was right
She had an open mind and she was so very kind
There ain't no blame in trying, there ain't no blame in trying
And he always wore a frown, just to bring that lady down

Well, the good and bad, four children yes they had
and oh it sad, what the good takes off the bad
But there ain't no living in crying, there ain't no living in crying
And when the light is a rest, evil's at it's best
It creeps all through the night and to the children is a fright
But there ain't no living in crying, there ain't no living in crying

And he always wore a frown, just to bring those children down

There came a day, bad news came her way
She didn't have long to live, but she had so much to give
There ain't no living in crying, no living in crying
And in the end, she pushed his hands away, yeah in the end
The lady had her say
There ain't no escaping like dying, no escaping like dying

Now he lives alone and that's the way it will stay
Until he's all ash and bone, until ole judgement day
To heaven he won't be flying, to heaven he won't be flying
Now when he frowns, he looks just like a clown
There ain't no one around, nobody to bring down

Way up above, there dwells a mother's love
Watching over the children from way up above
There ain't no living in crying, there aint' no living in crying
There ain't no living in crying

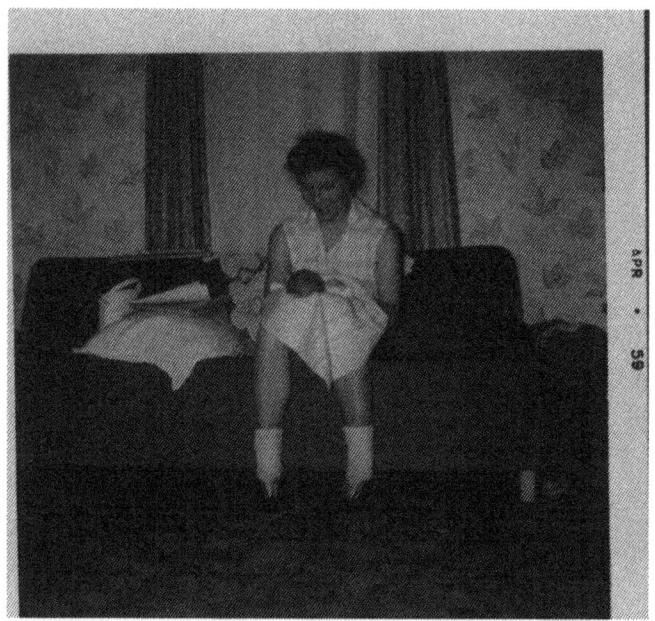

Mom was 19.....

Mom was nineteen when I was born. The joy of being a new mother is apparent as she looks down on me when I was one month old. It is so sad that there is no room for the sweet and innocent in this world.

My grandmother, Anna Erwin, holding me at around one month old. She was the epitome of the traditional grandmother and nothing like Al portrayed her to be. Grandma would run up and remove me from Al's lap when I was crying. Her mother's instincts had been telling her something, she just couldn't have imagined what. A woman should always trust her instincts because they are usually right.

Me and Al on Vine Street in El Dorado, Kansas. I was about three months old. Pretending to be the proud daddy, Al is typical of pedophiles. He looks harmless. Don't I look like a sex object? A father is supposed to be a protector and there is no forgiveness for those that strive to be hated and feared. I have never known a period of innocence or had a carefree childhood because my father stole every bit of it from me. I shall hate him even when worms ravage his body in the grave.

Once again Al—

Once again, Al puts on the proud daddy act, but he was mean to me whenever Mom left the room. He used the old, "You're my favorite" routine. Being the favorite of a child molester is no place of honor and they use many tricks to get close to a child. Another trick is to pretend to be looking for the soap while giving you a bath and miraculously, the soap is always near your sexual organs. When you live with the Bogey Man you don't have much to fear in the outside world.

Me and my great grandmother

Me and my great grandmother, Ethel Lawless in Moline, Kansas. I have many happy memories of being at their house. If we could have just stayed in Kansas with our support group my childhood could have been much different. If my great grandfather, Andy Lawless, would have known what my father was doing to us he would have loaded his shot gun and sent Al into the arms of the devil.

My aunt Sissy

My Aunt Phyllis (Sissy) and me in 1960. She was just a teenager then but already had bad feelings toward Allan Chadwick. Al tried hard to turn me against my aunt because he knew that she had a line on him. She could not have known just what was wrong with my father then.

My uncle Larry holds m

My uncle Larry holds me for the camera. As the first grandchild and niece I had plenty of fans. I used to fantasize about Larry beating the hell out of Al. He works construction and could well have done it. I would not want anyone going to jail for giving my father what he deserves. While the law cannot seem to do anything to Al, I'm sure that it would have no problem punishing those that try to stop him.

Mark, me and Al in Ft. Monmouth

Mark, me and Al in Fort Monmouth, New Jersey. It was here that Al first started throwing himself down the stairs. Whether it was for attention or a suicide attempt I am unclear. Unfortunately, there are more pictures of Al than Mom as she was usually the one taking pictures. The sexual abuse was in full force by this time. I remember hating myself and not wanting to play with the other kids because I felt like a mutation around them.

Looks like a good family

Looks like a good family, right? This was the first house we lived in on Okinawa. We were far away from those that could interfere with Al's plans and he started in on us with a vengeance. The car in the background is the one Al wrecked with Mark in the front seat. I never understood why Al didn't just kill himself instead of making us wish we had never been born. Specialist Sadist began to use anal penetration on Mark at this time. Mark looks just like any little boy, but Al had him painted as some wicked imp sent to ruin his life.

Sunday morning

Sunday morning. Don't we look happy? Al was in his twenties, but already appears and acts like a mean old man. I hated church by this time and had no use for a God that would sit and watch Al do horrible things to us. I did not see why I should pay homage to a God that sent daily messages to us that we were just pieces of meat who deserved no happiness.

I used to get out the picture

I used to get out the picture albums when I was depressed and wish I was back with grandma. Here we are seating on a slider at great grandma's house.

Mark and me around 1963

Mark and me around 1963. This was one of my mother's favorite pictures of us. Mark was a sweet, generous little boy, but Al tried to beat and rape the humanity right out of him. How many times must someone cry for help before being heard?

Playing at our first house

Playing at our first house on Okinawa. Most of the pictures were taken by my mother who wrote nice things about us on the backs. She was so pleased with us. It really felt like we lived with an angel and demon in the same household. There was no in between-the day was either bright and shiny or dark and stormy.

I'm pretending to be a soldier

I'm pretending to be a soldier inviting you to play cards. Both of us were into everything military. I am not sure why as Al was in the military and we hated everything about him. The main character in my thriller series, Harry Dolan, was a U.S. Army Ranger. I guess even as adults we still need heros.

Al and the son he hated

Al and the son he hated so intensely. Ironically, the cat statue on the post behind Al was to ward off evil spirits. Guess it didn't work.

An innocent little boy

An innocent little boy. Mark could do nothing right. Nothing. Al would use every opportunity to beat him and make him wish he had never been born. The more our mother interceded, the worst it became for Mark. Al would get his revenge one way or another. Both of us felt like we had been born twenty years old. By the time I graduated high school I was worn out from life and it seemed like I should be getting ready to retire, not just beginning adult life. Shame on the world that let Allan Chadwick inflict every sort of evil on his children. Al delighted in every failure Mark and I endured and each time we fell it made him feel more like a man. Of course, nothing he did to us contributed to our problems. We were just born losers. Al not only never went to jail, but out lived both his wife and oldest son.

Fishing at Moline

Fishing at Moline, Kansas. My aunt and cousin, Joe, are in the background. While I was abused as well as Mark, I didn't break any laws. Mark struck out against those that refused to help us and thus earned the wrath of society. Break into a school and go to jail, beat your son half to death and people do nothing. My deepest regret is that I did not tell my aunt and grandmother what was happening to us, but I really believed that Al could send my mother to prison. With the way the law is, I'm not so sure he could not have done just that.

Joyce and Al. Those that

Joyce and Al. Those that have been in abusive relationships know how easy it is to be fooled by a con artist. It can happen to anyone and no one needs to be throwing stones. My mother was young and naive and Al counted on that fact. Could you have made Al for a pedophile just by looking? Does he look mean to you? The police, social workers, counselors and probation officers through the years didn't think so either. Somewhere the devil is laughing hysterically at the fact that fate put a pedophile with a daycare teacher and then SHE is the one to suffer and die young, not good old Al.

All the Pretty Little Horses

Traditional

Hush a bye, don't you cry.
Go to sleep you little baby
         When you awake, you shall have
All the pretty little horses
Blacks and bays, dapples and grays
Coach and six little horses

Hush you bye and don't you cry
Go to sleepy baby
When you awake you shall have
all the pretty little horses

Way down yonder
In the meadow
Lies a poor little baby
Bees and the butterflies flutter around his eyes
And the poor little thing cries Mammy

Hush a bye don't you cry
Go to sleepy little baby
When you awake you shall have
All the pretty little horses

    This was one of my favorite songs as a child. It was simple and innocent and I had a passion for horses. A simple, delightful childhood was something totally alien to me.

On Vine Street

On Vine Street in El Dorado before leaving for Okinawa. Al had to go first to find a house, so we had a little reprieve. My aunt still remembers the apprehension she had the day we boarded the plane to San Francisco. She just had a feeling that something was wrong

Mark, Mom and me in Okinawa

Mark, Mom and me in Okinawa. Note the large tomb in the background. We used to play there and Mark found a skull one day when the door was open. The Japanese believe that the bones must be left intact or the spirit cannot go to heaven. It is the job of the oldest daughter to maintain the grave, but Mark and I did not know that and were very amused at the reaction to Mark bringing a skull outside. The island is full of such tombs. I am the only one still living of the three in the picture.

Joyce Chadwick standing outside her

Joyce Chadwick standing outside her classroom at the First Baptist Day Care. She was well liked by her students and their parents and very missed when she could not teach anymore. Mom took a leave of absence after teaching for sixteen years when she was diagnosed with cancer, February 1997. Thinking that she was going to return, Mom had made lesson plans for the whole next year. One of the hardest things I've ever had to do was go sort through her stuff at the day care. Mom also taught Sunday school for fourteen years. Al would rarely go to church with her, but starting going regularly after she died. There were those who thought that they had divorced years ago because he was never around. My biggest fear as a child was that Mom would die first, leaving us with just him and that is what happened. God and I still do not get along.

There is a water fountain dedicated to Mom in the El Dorado park where she used to take her students to play. It was her wish that the money from her memorial go to building a drinking fountain, so in a way children still benefit from Joyce's existence on earth.

Mark with his wife Tina

Mark with his wife, Tina, at their wedding. The years with Tina were the best of Mark's life and we all liked her. Tina encouraged Mark to return home as his health worsened to make amends with his family. She never dreamed that he would be treated with such disdain or would be abandoned by his father and youngest brother and sister. I could never have guessed at what would happen either, as Al turned out to be even more cruel than we already knew him to be and I am totally shocked at his influence over my remaining siblings. Al never did one nice thing for anybody that did not have an ulterior motive and he truly believes that money can buy everything and everybody.

Chapter Nine

Knee Jerk Reactions

Society is riddled with contradictions and child sexual abuse is no exception. While the local molester gets away with raping the kiddies, the law is busy trying to lock up parents who take pictures of the their children in their underwear. It is funny how pedophiles can possess pictures of kids in their drawers and cannot be arrested for it, but some over zealous prosecutor can send a young mother to jail for taking pictures of her own children. Think it does not happen? All across the world innocent people are facing charges for child pornography when all they did was take the same type of pictures their parents took of them. My mother took a picture of me when I was around two with my pants down around my ankles going to the grown up toilet for the first time. People are going to jail for the same type of photograph when the law is defending the rights of pedophiles to possess the very same pictures.

Sexual abuse accusations are also a favorite revenge tactic or useful in gaining custody of children. In 1992 I witnessed an extraordinary case in Kansas that made me feel like I had stepped into Nazi Germany. There was a young mother of three in MacPherson, Kansas who did not want to be on welfare, so she worked two jobs. She was also gay, which was all the ammo Social and Rehabilitation Services(SRS) needed. SRS was unhappy that, "Mary", was working all the time and never home with her children. Okay, that was a reasonable concern, but it so happened that the case-worker had some friends who wanted a healthy white daughter and were unable to produce one of their own. The couple, whom I'll call the Hoggs for this story, had not been able to adopt either. When Mary refused to go on welfare, SRS took the children and placed them in foster care. The two boys went one direction and the girl went with the friends of the social worker who wanted a daughter.

After some months of foster care, the girl began to tell stories of sexual abuse at home. Of course, these stories came about the time SRS formed a plan to return the children to Mary. The two boys denied that any type of abuse had occurred and they wished to go home. As the months went by the stories became better and better and the children were taken to therapists to determine what actually happened. I read the transcripts of the sessions and the baiting of the children was shameful. The two boys still said that nothing of the sort had happened to them. Mary was told by her lawyer that she would be arrested. Mary had obtained a lawyer to regain custody of her children when it was apparent that nothing she did was going to please SRS. Incredibly, the foster parents backed a truck up to Mary's house and removed all of the children's things and a few that did not belong to the children. The police said it was a domestic dispute and belonged in civil court. It seemed to be plain old burglary to me, but in MacPherson I guess it is okay for foster parents to steal from natural parents.

Mary went to the MacPherson County jail in spring of 1993. Her lawyer spent a total of fifteen minutes with her before her trial which took place months later. The bail was set so high that a Rockefeller would have had trouble making it, much less a single, poor mother of three. The children should have been brought to the jail to visit Mary, but they were not.

The foster parents had the children isolated except for occasional visits from their grandmother, who was met at a convenience store and not allowed to come up the Hogg's farm in outside of MacPherson. In July I received a letter from someone saying that Mary's lawyer had no intention of defending her, but would throw the case because he thought she was guilty. I filed a complaint on Mary's behalf with the disciplinary board, but trying to get anything done to a lawyer is like trying to prosecute a pedophile.

The abuse tales were so wild that no sensible cop or social worker should have bought it, but they not only bought it, they wrapped it up all nice in a package and sent Mary to prison. I told her lawyer that I had read the stories the children were telling before in true crime novels and that he should check it out. He did not. Mary's trial was three days of the worst load of blather imaginable in the free world. Her attorney called no witnesses, presented no evidence to show that she was not at home when the alleged abuse happened and did not believe that Mary needed any character witnesses.

The girl had told the story that her mother held orgies seven days a week in their home and that their father came up from Texas to join in as well. It was brilliant of the foster parents to eliminate the father from the picture too, wasn't it? It would not do much good to terminate the mother's parental rights with a natural father still walking around. Allegedly, the adults placed the three children in different rooms in the house and set an alarm clock for several minutes at a time. When the alarm went off, they would switch rooms and abuse a different child. This is a lovely story and one that I have read verbatim in a true crime book in the past. I guess the foster mother likes to read as much as I do! The foster parents covered every base. They made sure that Mary was not included in on the children's progress at school and even went so far as to place one of the children in special education without due process. Fortunately, I was an educational advocate and reported this transgression to the State Board of Education who had been told that the natural mother had no interest in her children.

The boys finally told the authorities what they wanted to hear when the cops explained that if the boys did not tell the truth like their sister, they would never go home. When they learned that bit of news, they decided to tell their own stories. The oldest boy also told a story that I had read before about a foster family in Texas. I had also been told this same story by a woman who experienced it, but again, Mary's lawyer didn't want to hear about it. The eldest son also came up with another story from a novel that I recognized and I gave the book to Mary's mother. It never seemed important to her attorney to point out the fact that SRS took the children from their home because Mary worked sixteen hours a day, yet at the same time, she could be home to put on elaborate orgies with people from all over the country and state wide.

The state's case consisted almost entirely of using the word "gay" as many times as the D.A. could work it into a sentence. They even trotted out a drag queen to testify that Mary was not a good mother. The fact that the guy had never seen any kind of abuse did not deter the jury from giving Mary a prison term of twenty to life. Three and a half years later Mary's case was overturned by the Kansas Court of Appeals, right when she was first eligible for parole. I recall the way the prosecutor joked around with the social worker and they both had a good laugh at the expense of the young woman they had set up. I would like to believe that this type of social worker is an exception in the system, but I know for a fact that he is not.

There was no apology from the State of Kansas and Mary's family is ruined. This case is an extreme example of how sexual abuse can be used as a weapon against the innocent, but one that needed to be mentioned. This case scared the hell out of me and everyone I knew at the time. It should scare the hell out of everyone who reads this book because it was not hard for authorities to destroy a young woman's life. If you are poor and not familiar with the law, you can be in serious trouble in this country. Shame on that jury for their verdict. They should have provided the checks and balances, but instead chose to use the court system to express their own prejudices. It is a travesty how social workers and lawyers can ruin people's lives and nothing is ever done to them. The judge napped through most of the trial.

Cases of false accusation cause discredit to those who are really being abused. When the public hears so many tales of sexual abuse it begins to turn a deaf ear just when sexual abuse has begun to be taken seriously. Putting everyone in jail but the correct people is not helping the problem. Investigators need to get all the facts instead of busting into the saloon with both barrels loaded and kill the piano player along with the outlaws.

It seems that society always has to go to extremes. I worked at a grade school where parents were having fits over a male kindergarten teacher. Their attitude seemed to be that no normal man would want to teach small children and thus he must have some ulterior motive. He turned out to be a good teacher and I enjoyed working in his room, but I know of a few parents who refused to let their children be in the man's class. Knee-jerk attitudes are not helping to eliminate pedophiles. In fact, pedophiles are contaminating the innocent who need to band together to stop the injustice. Catholic priests, gays and male grade school teachers need to stand together and put the blame for child abuse where it belongs-on pedophiles, who are especially adept at extending guilt to innocent people. Professional clowns should be concerned as well. It only takes one well known pedophile or child killer to taint a whole group of people.

It is a shame when a child is told to avoid priests because they are priests. Pedophiles are destroying our society little by little and now they have us not trusting the clergy. It is not the Catholic priesthood had makes pedophiles, but pedophiles are attracted to any lifestyle that involves authority, respect and access to children. There has also been scandal among the Amish communities. No one is immune to pedophiles and it is not surprising that pedophiles could be quite successful in a close knit religious sect, especially if that abuser holds a position of authority within that community. The blame should be placed on the criminal and not the lifestyle he chooses to contaminate. However, it is up to the religious community to stop tolerating those that rape children. There is no cure for pedophilia and clergy that rape children need to be defrocked and banished.

The religious right is only making things easier for pedophiles when they point fingers at gays and blame them for everything from the existence of cockroaches to the destruction of the family. Just how gays are destroying heterosexual family groups is a mystery to me and one that is not explained by those that preach such notions. Of course, they claim that only gays rape children, not the sacred heterosexual male. Sorry folks, but heterosexual males have been abusing their wives and children for centuries and that fact cannot be changed. It can be glossed over or down right ignored and the blame put on sneaky homosexuals in raincoats, but the fact is that most children are sexually abused by heterosexual male relatives. The problem needs to be fixed and not denied.

Another response to the reason for a decaying society is the lack of fathers in the home. I resent the notion that my grandmother did a lousy job of raising her children. What are mothers supposed to do when the men run out on them? A man in the home is not some magic bean. I wish my father had run off. Good father figures are needed, not just any old man in house like some groups are claiming. Two good parents are better than one, I agree. I just don't agree that one of them has to be a man and the other a woman. I would rather my mother had a relationship with another woman, if that woman had been kind to us and our mother, than to have suffered through the male/female marriage that she did. Children need peace, harmony, and kindness. Period. Everyone deserves some happiness.

Chapter Ten

Domestic Violence and Child Abuse Help

The following is a list of organizations that aid victims of domestic abuse. Even when a person is not actually physically abused, but verbally and emotionally tormented, there is still that fear of reprisal for disobeying. When a person feels that they are trapped and cannot leave a situation, that is kidnaping and unlawful arrest. Most women in dangerous relationships would not think of themselves as being arrested by their abusive partners, but if a police officer were to treat them the same way, that officer could be fired or disciplined. Do not underestimate the power of emotional abuse and it usually goes hand in hand with physical abuse. You cannot help you children, if you do not help yourself!

Alabama Coalition Against Domestic Violence
P.O. Box 4762

Montgomery, SL 36101
1-800-650-6522

Alaska Network on Domestic Violence and Sexual Assualt
130 Seward Street Room 209
Juneau, AK 99801
907-586-3650
Fax 907-463-4493

Arizona Coalition Against Domestic Violence
100 W. Camelback Rd. Suite 109
Phoenix, AR 85013
602-279-2900
Fax 602 279-2980 Email acadv@goodnet.com

Arkansas Coalition Against Domestic Violence
#1 Sheriff Lane Ste C
North Little Rock, AR 72114
501-812-0571
Fax 501-812-0578 Email ssigmon@arkansas.net

Coalition to End Domestic and Sexual Violence
2064 Eastman Ave, Ste 104
Ventura, CA 93003
805-654-8141
Fax 805-654-1264
24 hour hotline 805-656-1111
Spanish hotline 805-300-2181
TDD 805-656-4439

Statewide California Coalition for Battered Women
3711 Long Beach Blvd. Ste 718

Long Beach, CA 90807
Toll-free 888-SCCBW-52
Phone 562-981-1202
Fax 562-981-7067 Email Sccbw@sccbw.org

Colorado Domestic Violence Coalition
P.O. Box 18902
Denver, CO 80218
Toll free 888-778-7091
Phone 303-831-9632
Fax 303-832-7067 Email Ccadv@ix.netcom.com

D.C. Coalition Against Domestic Violence
513 U Street NW
Washington, DC 20001
202-783-5332
Fax 202-387-5684

My Sister's Place
P.O. Box 29506
Washington, DC 20017
24 hour hotline 202-529- 5991
Administrative office 202-529-5261

Delaware Coalition Against Domestic Violence
Box 847
Wilmington, DE 19899
Phone 302-658-2958
Fax 302-658-5049
24 hour bilingual line 888-522-2571

Florida Coalition Against Domestic Violence
308 East Park Ave

Tallahassee, FL 32301
Toll free 800-500-1119
Phone 850-425-2749
Fax 850-425-3091

Georgia Advocates for Battered Women and Children
250 Georgia Ave S.E. Ste 308
Atlanta, GA 30312
Toll free 800-334-2836
Phone 404-524-3847
Fax 404-524-959

Hawaii State Coalition Against Domestic Violence
98-939 Moanalua Road
Ajea, HI 96701
Phone 808-486-5072
Fax 808-486-5169

Iowa Coalition Against Domestic Violence
2603 Bell Ave Ste 100
Des Moines, IA 50321
Toll free 800-942-0333
Phone 515-244-8028
Fax 515-244-7417

Idaho Coalition Against Sexual and Domestic Violence
815 Park Blvd Ste 140
Boise, ID 83712
Toll free 888-293-6118

Phone 208-384-0419
Fax 208-331-0687 Email domvio@micron.net

Illinois Coalition Against Domestic Violence

801 South 11th Street
Springfield, IL 62703
217-789-2830
Fax 217-789-1939 Email ilcadv@springnet1.com

Friends of Battered Women and Their Children
P.O. Box 5185
Evanston, IL 60204
Phone 773-274-5232
Fax 773-274-2214
Hotline 1-800-603-HELP Email infor@afriendsplace.org

Life Span Police Domestic Violence
P.O. Box 445
Des Plaines, IL 60016
24 hour crises line 847-824-4454
Phone 847-824-0382
Fax 847-824-5311 Email life-span@life-span.org

Indiana Coalition Against Domestic Violence

2511 E. 46th Street Ste N-3
Indianapolis, IN 46205
Toll free 800-332-7385
Phone 317-543-3908
Fax 317-377-7050

Kansas Coalition Against Sexual and Domestic Violence
820 S.E. Quincy Ste 600
Topeka, KS 66612
Toll free 888-END-ABUSE State wide hot line
Phone 785-232-9784
Fax 785-232-9937

Kentucky Domestic Violence Association
P.O. Box 356
Frankfort, KY 40602
Phone 502-875-4132
Fax 502-875-4268

Louisiana Coalition Against Domestic Violence
P.O. Box 77308
Baton Rouge, LA 70879
Phone 225-752-1296
Fax 225-751-8927

Maine Coalition to End Domestic Violence
128 Main Street
Bangor, ME 04401
Phone 207-941-1194
Fax 207-941-2327

Maryland Network Against Domestic Violence
6911 Laurel Bowie Road Ste 309
Bowie, MD 20715
Toll free 800-MD-HELPS
Phone 301-352-4575
Fax 301-809-0422

Jane Doe Inc. Massachusetts Coalition Against Sexual Assault and Domestic Violence
14 Beacon Street Ste 507
Boston, MA 02108
Phone 617-248-0922
Fax 617-248-0902

Bay County Women's Center
P.O. Box 1458
Bay City, MI 48706
Toll free 800-834-2098
Phone 517-686-4551
Fax 517-686-0906

Michigan 24 hour Crisis Line 517-256-6776

Minnesota Coalition of Battered Women
450 N. Syndicate Street Ste 122
St. Paul, MN 55104
Metro Area Hotline 651-646-0994
Phone 651-646-6177
Fax 651-646-1527 Email mcbw@pclink.com

Missouri Coalition Against Domestic Violence
415 E. McCarty Street
Jefferson City, MO 65101
Phone 573-634-4161
Fax 573-636-3728

Women's Support and Community Services
2838 Olive Street

St. Louis, MO 63103
Hotline 314-531-2003
Office 314-531-9100

Mississippi State Coalition Against Domestic Violence
P.O. Box 4703
Jackson, MS 39296
Toll free 800-898-3234
Phone 601-981-9196
Fax 601-981-2501 Email mcadv@misnet.com

Crisis Line
P.O. Box 6644
Great Falls, MT 59406
Phone 406-453-HELP
Toll free 1-888-587-0199

Montana Coalition Against Domestic and Sexual Violence
P.O. Box 633
Helena, MT 59624
Phone 406-443-7794
Fax 406-443-7818

Nebraska Domestic Violence and Sexual Assault Coalition
825 M Street Ste 404
Lincoln, NE 68508
Toll free 800-876-6238
Phone 402-476-6256
Fax 402-476-6808

Nevada Network Against Domestic Violence
100 W. Grove Ste 315
Reno, NV 89509
Toll free 800-500-1556
Phone 775-828-1115
Fax 775-828-9991

SAFE House
Sunrise Drive Ste G-70
Henderson, NV 89014
Phone 702-451-4203
Fax 702-451-4302 Email safe@intermind.net

New Hampshire Coalition Against Domestic and Sexual Violence
Box 353
Concord, NH 03302
Toll free 800-852-3388 (In New Hampshire)
Helpline 603-225-9000 (outside NH)
Phone 603-224-8893
Fax 603-228-6096

New Jersey Coalition for Battered Women
2620 Whitehorse/Hamilton Square Rd
Trenton, NJ 08690
Toll free for battered lesbians 800-224-0211(NJ only)
Phone 609-584-8107
Fax 609-584-9750
TTY 609-584-0027

Strengthen Our Sisters
Box U
Hewitt, NJ 07421

Email ssisters@warwick.net
24 hour hotline 973-728-0007

New Mexico State Coalition Against Domestic Violence
Box 25266
Albuquerque, NM 87125
Toll free 800-773-3645 (NM only)
Legal helpline 800-209-DVLH
Phone 505-246-9240
Fax 505-246-9434   Email nmcadv@nmcadv.org

New York State Coalition Against Domestic Violence
79 Central Ave
Albany, NY 12206
Toll free 800-942-6909
Phone 518-432-4864
Fax 518-463-3155

North Carolina Coalition Against Domestic Violence
301 W. Main Street
Durham, NC 27701
Phone 919-956-9124
Fax 919-682-1449

North Dakota Council on Abused Women's Services
State Networking Office
418 East Rosser Ave Ste 400
Bismark, ND 58501
Toll free 800 472-2911(ND only)
Phone 701-255-6240
Fax 701-255-1904

Ohio Domestic Violence Network
4041 North High St. Ste 400
Columbus, OH 43214
Toll free 800-943-9840
Phone 614-784-0023
Fax 614-784-0033

Oklahoma Coalition Against Domestic Violence and Sexual Assault
2525 NW Expressway Ste 208
Oklahoma City, OK 73116
Toll free 800-522-9054
Phone 405-848-1815
Fax 405-848-3469

Oregon Coalition Against Domestic and Sexual Violence
520 N.W. Davis Ste 310
Portland, OR 97209
Toll free 800-622-3782
Phone 503-223-7411
Fax 503-223-7490

Pennsylvania Coalition Against Domestic Violence/National Resource Center on D.V.
6440 Flank Drive Ste 1300
Harrisburg, PA 17112
Toll free 800-932-4632
Phone 717-545-6400
Fax 717-545- 9456

Rhode Island Coalition Against Domestic Violence
422 Post Road Ste 202

Warwick, RI 02888
Toll free 800-494-8100
Phone 401-467-9940
Fax 401-467-9943

South Carolina Coalition Against Domestic Violence and Sexual Assault
Box 7776
Columbia, SC 29202
Toll free 800-260-9293
Phone 803-256-2900
Fax 803-256-1030

South Dakota Coalition Against Domestic Violence and Sexual Assualt
Box 141
Pierre, SD 57501
Toll free 800-572-9196
Phone 605-945-0869
Fax 605-945-0870

South Dakota Network Against Family Violence and Sexual Assualt
1-800-430-SAFE

Tennessee Task Force Against Domestic Violence
Box 120972
Nashville, TN 37212
Toll free 800-356-6767
Phone 615-386-9406
Fax 615-383-2967

Texas Council on Family Violence
Box 161810
Austin, TX 78716

Toll free 800-525-1978
Phone 512-794-1133
Fax 512-794-1199

Families in Crisis
Box 25
Killeen, TX 76540
Phone 212-634-1184
Toll free 888-799-SAFE

Domestic Violence Advisory Council
120 North 200 West
Salt Lake City, UT 84103
Toll free 800-897-LINK
Phone 801-538-4100
Fax 801-538-3993

Women Helping Battered Women
Phone 802-658-1996
Toll free 800-228-7395

Women's Rape Crisis Center
800-489-7273

Vermont Network Against Domestic Violence and Sexual Assualt
Box 405
Montpelier, VT 05601
Phone 802-223-1302
Fax 802-223-6943   Email vnadvsa@sover.net

Virginia Family Violence and Sexual Assault Hotline

2850 Sandy Bay Road Ste 101
Williamsburg, VA 23185
Toll free 800-838-VADV
Phone 757-221-0990
Fax 757-229-1553

Washington State Coalition Against Domestic Violence
8645 Martin Way NE Ste 103
Lacey, WA 98516
Phone 360-407-0756
Fax 360-407-0761
TTY 360-407-0767   Email wscadv@cco.net

Washington State Domestic Violence Hotline
Toll free 800-562-6025
Email csn@willapabay.org
West Virginia Coalition Against Domestic Violence

Elk Office Center
4710 Chimney Dr Ste A
Charleston, WV 25203
Phone 304-965-3552
Fax 304-965-3572

Manitowoc Domestic Violence Center
Box 1142
Manitowoc, WI 54220
Phone 920-684-5770

Wisconsin Coalition Against Domestic Violence

1400 E. Washington Ave Ste 232
Madison, WI 53703
Phone 609-255-0539
Fax 608-255-3560

National Battered Women's Law Project
275 7th Ave Ste 1206
New York, NY 10001
Phone 212-741-9480
Fax 212-741-6438

Battered Women's Justice Project (For battered women charged with crimes) c/o National Clearinghouse for the Defense of Battered Women
125 S. 9th Street Ste 302
Philadelphia, PA 19107
Toll free 800-903—0111
Phone 215-351-0010
Fax 215-351-0779

National Network to End Domestic Violence
666 Pennsylvania Ave SE Ste 303
Washington, DC 20003
Phone 202-543-5566
Fax 202-543-5626

Child Abuse Hotlines

Childhelp USA National Child Abuse Hotline
1-800-4-A-CHILD
TDD 800-2-A-CHILD

Alaska
800-478-4444

Arizona
888-SOS-CHILD

Arkansas
800-482-5964

Connecticut
800-842-2288

Delaware
800-292-9582

Florida
800-962-2873

Illinois
800-252-2873

Indiana
800-562-2407

Iowa
800-362-2178

Kansas
800-922-5330

Kentucky
800-752-6200

Maine
800-452-1999

Maryland
Call local law enforcement or
County Dept. of Social Services

Massachusetts
800-792-5200

Michigan
800-942-4357

Mississippi
800-222-8000

Missouri

Montana

800-392-3738   800-332-6100

Nevada   New Hampshire
800-992-5757   800-894-5533

New Jersey   New Mexico
800-792-8610   800-797-3260
TDD 800-835-5510

New York   North Carolina
800-342-3720   800-662-7030

North Dakota   Oklahoma
800-245-3736   800-522-3511

Oregon   Pennsylvania
800-854-3508   800-932-0313

Rhode Island   Texas
800-742-4453   800-252-5400

Utah   Virginia
800-768-9399   800-552-7096

Washington   West Virginia
800-562-5624   800-352-6513

  Wyoming
800-457-3659

Chapter Eleven

Crutches and Crowns

When trying to survive a bad situation there are many things that can be used to cushion the pain. Mark and I had great imaginations and made up movie scripts, then acted the story out. I had a passion for music and wrote songs, painted pictures and built models, but one of the devices that really helped us to endure the presence of Allan Chadwick, was humor. We loved *MAD* magazine and owned all of them from the sixties and seventies. I'm not sure if we already had a strange sense of humor or the magazine created it.

I learned to love music when a salesman came around to our apartment in Tyler Gardens and convinced my mother that I was a prodigy. Unfortunately, the guy sold accordions. While I liked to play the big one hundred and twenty bass accordion in private, it was not something that I liked to brag about. Who was I supposed to emulate? Lawrence Welk? I've yet to meet a ten year old who wants to be associated with polka dancers and Polly Anna type wholesomeness. Every year I asked for a guitar, but only received plastic ones. When I finally did get a wood guitar

I was fourteen. I scrutinized the Christmas packages around the tree, but could see nothing shaped like a guitar. Christmas morning, to my horror, the guitar had been under the tree. I know my mother meant well, but I could have died when I saw that tiny little box with small children on the front. It was a beginner's instrument that had colored dots on the fingerboard. I placed the thing in my closet and tried to ignore it. Of course, the neighborhood kids asked it I got a guitar for Christmas and I admitted it the first few times, but then lied and said that I did not when I couldn't take the strange looks of my comrades any longer.

On my fifteenth birthday Al asked if I wanted a real guitar and of course I replied that I did-the memories of that kiddie toy still burnt my ego. We took the accordion to a pawn shop and traded it for a guitar. I was happy, but my mother never really got over it. She would joke around and say, "I don't want to talk about it." when the topic of the exchange came up, but I know it bothered her. While I desperately wanted a guitar, I knew Al didn't do it for me, but for the hurt it would cause my mother. Usually, I would never have done anything that would upset my mother, but I was fifteen in a world with Jefferson Airplane and I owned an accordion! Need I say more?

I wrote my first song the same night I traded the old accordion for the guitar. It turned out to be a real savior for me and provided some limelight in my other wise un-notable high school career. Art and music gave me an outlet that Mark did not have. Mark later became an avid reader of fantasy and adventure novels, but as a child he had not figured out how to compensate for the dyslexia. There was no place for the frustration and rage to go but out. I can say one thing for misery and unhappiness-they lend great things to creativity and my best work was accomplished from around age fifteen to thirty. Not that I wouldn't have traded fathers in an instant because I would have, artistic talents or not.

When you spend your childhood in a fog of abuse you must find some way to maintain sanity. Everyone has some talent or interest that could provide a crutch in which to hobble through the tender years and if you're lucky, you could turn that crutch into a crown to wear proudly. I grew weary of playing in bars and coffee houses, so no talent scout from a record company ever found me. My passion for art mellowed through the years, but I still have a passion for writing. There is nothing wrong if your talent is never rewarded with a crown, it is yours. No one can take abilities from you, even though abusers try very hard to smother the life out of you. Remember this-if your abuser targets something that you do for ridicule, it means you' re good at it and they are terrified that you will one day out shine them. One day you will be out from under their sadistic control and then they will have no reason for living.

The day Mark was being thrown into the street by his father, a couple from his church came to the house to give him some support. The woman was a Holocaust survivor and she said to Mark, " I remember when the Nazis did this to us. They came into our home, threw us out and took everything for themselves." It was one of those classic moments that no fiction writer could improve upon. Holocaust survivors have much to teach victims of abuse as they lived through the worst that humans can do to other humans. The Jewish Defense League has the motto, "Never Again" and it is one that I take to heart. No one group of people should ever be targeted for torture and elimination(with the exception of sex offenders). Children are people too and the damage done to them by pedophiles can equal anything done by the Nazis and sometimes pedophiles kill their victims as well.

One of the motivations for concentration camp inmates to survive was so that they could tell the story and stop it from happening again. It should be one of a sexually abused child's goals as well. Live to shout the dirty little secrets from the roof tops how ever you can. Pour out that anger and rage in art, music, writing or become a prosecutor or police officer so that you may aid in ceasing the activity of pedophiles. Do not let abusers ruin what is left of your life because nothing would made them happier. Turn your horror into something positive and don't let it set there and rot your soul.

Mark came to the conclusion that if there were guardian angels, then there were angels on the other side as well. These beings were called Dicksmack angels. They look like middle-aged, potbellied men, wear loin clothes with no shirts and carry around maggot wands. The wands are shaped like a dildo because they are waved over people to screw up their lives. Young ones have wings, but not like the more experienced Dicksmacks who have ruined enough lives to have earned their Penis Wings. Their wings will have little dick heads all along the crests. Mark asked me to visualize these beings on paper and I did so. I'm sure that I have several perched on my roof all the time given the luck that I possess!

There are those up tight persons who will see no humor in such things or will not allow their kids to read this book, but if your child has already been used by a pedophile that seems pretty pointless. There is something about rape that kills you from the inside out. You do not get over it, not completely. Whatever it takes for a child to cope should be tolerated within reason. Setting fires, killing small animals or the abuser are not appropriate. It amazes me how the law cannot seem to punish the abusers, but have no trouble jailing victims who cannot tolerate it any longer. No child should do prison time for striking back at their rapist. Live long enough to destroy his reputation and then disown him.

When you tell and it gets you no where, use your crutches to survive. Try to be excellent at something and don't look back at the devil on your tail. Keep moving forward and enjoy what you can in life. If you are lucky enough to have one good parent then soak up what kindness you can. It's one wicked ride and sometimes you cannot get off when it would do you the most good.

As I got older I learned to turn Al off. He would try to make us all depressed and unhappy, but my mother would over ride him. For what-ever reasons that my mother did not divorce her husband, she bent over backwards trying to make up for what he had done to us. She was thrilled at every little present given to her, always tried to make every holiday and birthday special, was a den mother, taught Sunday school and worked at a day care for years to pay for Mark being at Menninger's. If Al tried to throw fits or bring everybody down with his "hemorrhoid" look, Mom would suggest we go fishing or do something else to ignore him. Mom knew she could not erase the past with me and Mark, but she was going to make sure that the youngest children knew no such pain.

Mom liked to do crafts and used to get one every month in the mail. If she didn't like the one that came, I did it. She used to read historical novels by the sackful and liked to sew. You do what you can when you do not believe that escape is possible. I don't know how she did it, but Mom never became cynical or full of rage like Mark and me. She really believed that there is good in everyone and could find brightness in every situation. I do not understand why someone who loved life as much as my mother had to die a painful death at age fifty -eight, while Al lives on.

There is someone that thinks Joyce deserved it and never places flowers on her grave, but he is also a self righteous, right-wing hypocrite that preaches against divorce, so what was Joyce to have done then? The man rules the household no matter what and the woman has to stay with him period. Her life is to revolve around him regardless of what he does or does not do. It is just that sort of sick attitude that laid the foundation for Al's campaign in the first place. He even tells lies about how our mother beat and starved us, yet pays homage to our pedophile father and allows his children to visit Al. The only people who defend pedophiles are other pedophiles and anyone who allows their children to be around one deserves a jail cell. If you cannot learn from experiences, then what good is living? What purpose is there for human kind if the same mistakes are made again and again and again? Mark, Mom and me suffered the worst of Al's abuse and there is no reason that abuse should continue in the Chadwick family. No excuse at all. I did not put the child abuse survival crown on my head just so I could hand it down to the next generation. It should be placed on a shelf and the story told, but never worn again.

I turned my rage against my father in an adventure series featuring a man named Harry Dolan. Harry does everything to pedophiles that I want to do and does not get caught. Harry is one way I turned a crutch into a crown. While I am not on the best seller list, I am in print and our story is told to the world. Mark nearly cried when he first saw the book and said it was the only justice that we would ever know. There will be at least one more Harry book as Mark and I discussed the plot for it before he died. I also have to write a third book because of the many victims who have responded to my web site, *Silence is a Pedophile's Lethal Weapon*. On the site Harry has his own mailbox where victims can tell him what they want Harry to do to pedophiles. The amount of pain and anger of the sexually abused out there is gut wrenching, but I can ease it some by allowing Harry to extract their revenge for them.

The best revenge victims of domestic abuse can inflict on their abusers is to survive and thrive. Grow stronger and leave that loser behind. Another woman who has used her writing skills to expose her pedophile father is Susan Kesegich. She told her story in the book *Twisted Roots of Evil.* Her father, Hubert, got away with abusing his first family and actually started in on another! My father had the exact same intentions after my mother died, but we ruined that for him. Susan tells a horrifying tale of abuse and so similar to my own it is scary, but as Harry Dolan says, "God has one asshole mold, they just all get different paint jobs". *Twisted Roots of Evil* is an excellent example of throwing light on dark places. The author is very active in the prevention of child abuse and if everyone would start screaming as loud as we have, then maybe the law would stop playing nice with child rapists.

One of the best examples of pulling out of a bad situation is the story of Tina Turner. Born Anna Mae Bullock, Turner began life with all the usual hopes of a young woman leaving home for the first time. Her innocence and naivety were beaten out of her by her husband, Ike Turner. Tina Turner poured all of her pain and anger into her music which was something that Ike could not take from her, even though he tried during the divorce when he kept all the publishing rights and royalties. Tina took nothing from her hard years with Ike Turner but her name, yet she took that little bit of sunshine and lit up the world with it. She is an inspiration to anyone who has doubts about whether they could make it without their abuser. Not everyone will become an enormous success like Tina Turner, but they can find themselves again and take back their lives.

Mark worked as a medical technician in the Boston area where he treated the elderly with kindness and I adopted a severely handicapped teenager. We have tried to alleviate some of the suffering in the world and repair the tears in our souls at the same time. It is a never ending struggle to not become cruel and selfish like those that live to teach such lessons. When I look around I see the bad people of the world suffering very little, if at all and those that would give their last bread crumb to a stranger know nothing but hardship. I would like to believe the old philosophy that you reap what you sow, but I know that it is not true. Not for rapists anyway. The best way to deal with child abuse is to prevent it or stop it early on.

When all seems hopeless, try to think of something funny about the abuser. There must be some instant when he or she looked stupid or was humiliated. One of my favorite memories is the time we were going down the New Jersey Turnpike during a blizzard. We had just had breakfast and was on the road once again heading for Kansas. It came upon us slowly at first. Mark looked at me and I at him. Mom peered into the back seat then turned to Al while she rolled the window down. She informed him that he would never, ever eat pancakes while we were on the road again. Once

Mom rolled her window down, we all did, to release the horrid butt air Al had generated with pancakes and syrup. I'm sure that the people around us wondered why in the hell that station wagon was traveling through a blizzard with all the windows down-now they know!

Those that are trapped in an abusive situation need to find joy and light where ever it can be found. Do not let the monster in your life ruin every aspect of living because they would love nothing more. As a child I had a passion for animals, especially horses and dogs. If your abuser won't let you have a pet, then enjoy the ones that roam the neighborhood. Love music, but can't play anything? That's okay too. There is enough music being produced today that there will be something that you can lose yourself in. Another good thing to do to keep your sanity is the find a pen pal who lives far away. Their letters can remind you that there is another world out there and a life of darkness is not permanent.

Grab onto any rope you can until you are old enough to leave home or too old for the abuser to have any interest in you. Forget suicide, as tempting as the relief may seem. It is not an answer and will only leave the abuser free to victimize those you leave behind. You could hope that you are reincarnated into a better life, but there is always the chance that there is no afterlife or you could trade your present life for one that is worse-and there is always something worse. When you sit and imagine putting a gun to your head or over dosing on pills also imagine the joy you will provide to the abuser once your tainted little butt is out of the picture. Make no mistake, that is exactly how the abuser sees you. You are a constant reminder of the nasty things you know about him, a walking indictment of the criminal that he is, so don't reward him with your death.

Chapter Twelve

What Should be Done to Sex Offenders?

According to the vast majority of people who email Harry Dolan, rapists need to be either castrated or killed. I tend to agree, but most victims of rape do. I can hear the gasps from the bleeding hearts as I write this chapter. But rape isn't about sex, so why do we have to cut off their genitals? The only people who think that rape is not about sex have never been raped. If it wasn't about sex first and foremost, then no penis would be involved. It is about sex because forced sex is the most personal way to humiliate a person, do permanent damage and get off all at the same time. You can get your jollies and most likely never do prison time because your lawyer can make the kid or woman out to be sluts asking for it. Convicting a sex offender is harder than convicting a murderer, especially if the victims are elderly women or children.

I cannot imagine why anyone would defend a rapist's right to keep his weapon. Other felons are not allowed to keep theirs, so why the rapist?

Because the society we live in has advanced no more that the phallus wor-shiping tribes of times past. In this society, soft drink companies think it is funny to have old men on erection stimulating drugs get boners over singers young enough to be their great-granddaughters. It really isn't sur-prising that people want to keep the ole wang out of the garbage disposal. This world gave the Nobel Prize for Medicine to a pill for limp dick! It must have been a real blow to those thriving to cure cancer and heart dis-ease. Sorry, but your work pales in comparison to a pill that can make an eighty year old man get a hard on!

There are those that would argue that cutting off an offender's penis and testicles would just make him mad and he would turn to other forms of violence. Wrong. I have seen for myself what happens to pedophiles who have all of their parts removed in prison and they are no longer a threat to anyone. The rapist spends the rest of his life with just a little tube sticking out near the former location of his penis-his reason for living eliminated. If my own father was castrated he would want to die and I cannot imagine a better punishment, aside from execution, for a rapist. Sex offenders lives orbit around their dicks and it really isn't much more complicated than that fact. There is no cure for rape. Once a rapist, always a rapist.

Of course, there are many shrinks and bleeding hearts who will disagree with me. These are the same people who object to rapists going from prison to a psychiatric facility for crimes they might commit. They will re-offend, not might, but will. I hold the motivations of those who defend sex offenders highly suspect, especially those that victimize children and the elderly. If it were up to some, Megan's Law would be appealed and the poor rapists could once again go back to living undetected and thus free to browse leisurely for victims.

Hiding their dirty little secrets is how rapists past their depravity from one generation to the next. If it were up to me, sex offenders would be physically castrated and an "R" tattooed onto their foreheads for all to see. "But then they can't start over again!", whine the bleeding hearts. That is exactly the whole point. They cannot start over again ruining people's lives and that is a rapist's only intentions. Having a criminal record does not stop pedophiles from finding others to abuse either, as many will take jobs in nursing homes to make do with the elderly if they are not allowed around children. If rapists had no penis or testicles, they wouldn't look for sexual release. Sympathy is wasted on those that rape other people and those that defend their rights sicken me.

I have worked as a correctional officer in Kansas at a maximum security prison. The majority of the inmates were violent offenders and sex offenders. They all could play the system like a rare old violin and make authorities dance anything from jigs to a waltz. The facility was fairly new, very clean and air conditioned. The inmates had cable and HBO for free. My grandmother could not afford to have premium channels as many seniors cannot, yet if you murder or rape someone you get it free of charge. The inmates get two free letters a week courtesy of the taxpayers as well as free legal correspondence regardless of the cost. There was a enormous air conditioned gym and room for crafts where inmates could make products to sell. If they needed medical treatment for any reason it was free. Heart surgery, chemotherapy, dialysis are all free to a criminal even if that criminal has a life sentence. So much for "the rest of your natural life" in prison sentences.

To be paroled inmates need to impress the parole board which means being involved in a work program, therapy and religion. Freedom of Religion gives inmates excuses to do activities they would never have any interest in on the outside or an opportunity to wear gang jewelry. There was one inmate who converted to Judaism just so he could wear the six pointed star that was the symbol of his gang. Inmates put on a good act around the officers, medical staff, corrections counselors and ministers, but they let it all hang out in their correspondence. Church groups like to bring religious cassette tapes to inmates in segregation believing that they are reaching the poor soul, but all they are doing is providing a means for one felon to communicate with another. They place scotch tape over the hole in the tape so that they can record over the pious message for their own use.

One minister gave an award to an inmate for his spiritual progress. The same inmate who had impressed the minister with his sanctimonious behavior was sending child pornography cartoons to his pedophile friends. In spite of all society does to rehabilitate sex offenders nothing works. While they manage to fool the parole board and religious communities, rapists are only waiting for the day they can resume their predatory behavior. There was another inmate who had impressed a minister so much that he convinced the man sponsor his parole in a very small town. This inmate also had a pen pal girlfriend with a nine year old daughter in that town. She kept asking him why he only called the house when the little girl was the only one at home. I wonder?

The worst crimes the inmate commits, the larger his fan club. Women write to these cold hearted murders and rapists explaining how they grew up being sexually abused and beaten and how they hope to start a new lives. Of course, the inmates are more than happy to tell these women whatever they wish to hear as long as they are willing to send money every week. Some of these women have small children, yet want to offer their homes to violent felons for parole. One inmate was convicted of murdering thirty-six women and he had at least three of his pen pals move to El Dorado, Kansas just so they could be near him. He thoroughly insulted one of these women for spending her money on moving expenses instead of sending it to him. Others threaten to beat their old mothers if a money order does not accompany their letter.

The point to all of this is simple; prison is no punishment and it does nothing to change rapists and murderers. There are people in this world who are just plain evil and all the therapy and religion in the world are not going to change it. Pedophiles are the worst of them all because they create the personalities that populate the prisons and make others willing victims. Chickenhawks are not only protected in society, but in prison as well. What is the problem here? Let them fend for themselves against grown men and maybe then they will understand what it is to be a child who is raped.

Chemical castration is a waste of time and taxpayer money. Our prisons are full because there are no real consequences for brutal acts. We were told to treat inmates like five year olds and tell them to do something several times before writing them up. Why? Why on earth do I owe a violent felon anything? If pedophiles and adult rapists knew they would have their genitals removed for their actions, they would think very hard before raping anyone. Is that so bad? We could return to boiling pedophiles in oil or drawing and quartering rapists the way they used to deal with sex offenders, how about that?

For those that think my views are jaded and not realistic, the U.S. Department of Justice has information that verifies my pessimistic view of sex offenders and the need to get them stopped. In a study published in March of 1996 the Department of Justice found that inmates who had victimized a child were usually older than adult victimizers and less likely to have a criminal record. Violent child offenders were much more likely to have been sexually or physically abused as children and nearly seventy percent of them white males. Offenders that victimize children tend to receive lighter sentences than those who assault adults. Three Quarters of the violent assaults against children took place in the child's home or the offenders and a third committed the crime against their own child. In the 1991 *Survey of Inmates in State Correctional Facilities,* it was found that nearly two thirds of rapists and sexual assaulters committed their crimes against children. Four in ten inmates convicted for forcible sodomy committed those crimes against children under eighteen. Over half of the violent child offenders had victims under age twelve. Inmates who assaulted children twelve and under accounted for nearly ninety percent of those serving sentences for child abuse.

Offense	% of Victims Age 12 or Less	% of Victims Ages 13 to 17
All Violent Offenses	100.0%	100.00%
Homicide	9.0%	10.3%
Murder	6.8%	8.9%
Negligent Manslaughter	2.2%	1.4%
Kidnaping	2.0%	3.18%
Rape and Sexual Assault	75.4%	66.3%
Forcible Rape	11.7%	18.6%
Forcible Sodomy	3.1%	2.6%
Statutory Rape	1.8%	1.4%
Lewd Acts with Children	37.2%	31.9%
Robbery	3.2%	9.6%
Assault	9.7%	10.4%
Aggravated Assault	4.9%	8.6%
Child Abuse	4.5%	.7%
Simple Assault	.2%	.3%

Other Violent Offenses	.7%	.3%
Number of Inmates	33, 287	26,998

Offenders convicted of child violence are more likely to be white, older and to had been married in comparison to adult victimizers. White inmates were three times as likely than black inmates to have had a child victim-around twenty-seven percent of white inmates incarcerated for violent crimes committed those offenses against children. What this information means to the average person is that we are worried about the wrong people in everyday life. The scary looking single, young black man hanging out on the corner is much less likely to harm your child than the forty year old, white married accountant living next door to you. You should be worried about the married man who is coaching your child's baseball team, not the gay man who might be a scout leader. For some reason, white heterosexual males are more likely to be sexual predators than any other group. They are also more likely to have grown up in a home with two parents and to have been sexually abused as a child in comparison with black inmates and adult offenders.

No. Of Parents Grew Up with	Child Victimizers		Adult Victimizers	
	White	Black	White	Black
Single Parent	25%	55%	34%	53%
Both Parents	63%	30%	53%	31%
Other	12%	15%	13%	16%

On any given day of the week in 1994, 234,000 of those convicted of rape or sexual assault were under the care of, in custody or under control of the department of corrections in the fifty states. Sixty percent of those offenders were on parole or probation. Twenty four percent of those serving time for rape were on parole or probation when convicted for a sexual offense.

Those that still think we can afford to coddle pedophiles need to consider that 95% of child victimizers report they were physically or sexually abused as children. Half of the violent offenders with a history of child abuse victimized children and they are twice as likely to have suffered sexual or physical abuse as children than those with adult victims. The majority who reported being abused as children stated that the offender was someone they knew and half said the abuse was committed by a parent or guardian. While many adult offenders claim to have been under the influence of drugs or alcohol when committing crimes a very low percentage of child victimizers make that claim.

Who Abused the Offenders	% of Violent Offenders with Child Victims
No Abuse	15.5%
Stranger	24.5
Parent/guardian	32.4
Other Relative	46.6
Acquaintances	43.1

Those that victimize children tend to get lighter sentences than those who commit offenses against adults, except for the crimes of murder, kidnaping and negligent manslaughter. Some of the reasons for the more lenient sentences are the fact that child victimizers tend to not have prior criminal histories and they are less likely to use weapons as a show of force. Pedophiles just seem to have it made. Inmates who committed crimes against a child were more likely to have multiple victims and the most likely to be serving time for aggravated assault, negligent manslaughter and murder. Here is something for thought-the 60,000 state prison inmates who committed violent crimes against children may have had up to 95,000 victims. This information is according to *The 1991 State Survey of Inmates in State Correctional Facilities.*

Three-fourths of the child victims of violent crimes were female and almost a third were the offender's own child or a step-child. Most of those that victimize children know the child and are of the same race as the child. It is very dangerous to be a child in a "normal" family.

	Stranger	Acquaintance	Own Child	Other Family
Total	100%	100%	100%	100%
Murder	13.6	6.8	5.0	5.7
Rape	13.5	6.0	18.8	13.3
Sexual Assault	38.6	64.7	61.5	73.7
Robbery	7.2	1.1	0.5	1.1
Assault	12.8	8.5	11.1	3.9
All Other	14.3	2.9	3.1	2.3

Most inmates who committed violent crimes against children did so either in the child's home or the offender's. Sixty percent of adult violent offenders felt a need to go elsewhere to commit their offenses. Pedophiles can commit crimes for years without ever being caught because they can simply just shut the door whenever they feel like raping a child. Once in a while though, my own father would take us out into the woods if he thought there was too much risk at home.

	Home			
	Victim's	Offender's		Public Place
Total	100%	100%		100%
Murder	9.2	3.6		15.5
Negligent Manslaughter	.7	1.1		8.0
Rape	15.7	15.6		12.6
Sexual Assault	58.7	68.4		35.1
Robbery	4.9	1.6		6.6
Assault	8.0	8.4		18.8
Other crimes	2.8	1.3		3.4

Forty-eight percent of the women incarcerated in jails throughout the U.S. in 1994 reported being physically or sexually abused prior to admission and twenty-seven percent reported being raped. Predators create more predators and victims so that the cycle never ends. If the reader cares about nothing at all, but tax dollars, then they should realize that America cannot afford sex offenders any longer. They are spreading rot from one generation to the next.

According to the Uniform Crime Reporting Program of the F.B.I., of all the victims of sex offenders, two thirds are under the age of eighteen and fifty-eight percent under the age of twelve. Ninety percent of those under twelve knew their offenders. Rape victims from the ages of 18 to 29 had a prior relationship with the rapist. It isn't the stranger on the street preying on women and children, but daddy, Uncle Harvey or that nice man hanging out at the club on Saturday night.

Nothing in my research or experiences has convinced me that castrating sex offenders is not the solution. The punishment needs to fit the crime. Letting pedophiles lay around a prison cell making child porn from little girl's underwear ads isn't doing the job. Allowing someone like Allan Chadwick to rape whom ever he chooses as long as he is related to them is wrong. The only way Al will ever stop thinking about sexually abusing children is to remove his genitals and that is the only way.

People that still do not have a problem with child sex offenders need to consider how often that crime leads to murder. The incident-level data collected by the F.B.I. in 1994 indicated that eleven percent of all murder victims were children and half of those between the ages of fifteen and seventeen. There is no doubt in my mind that my father killed children in Korea and Vietnam, if he could have strangled us and gotten away with it he would have done it. He thought Jonbenet Ramsey asked for what she got as she was a little whore. Wonder why he never called Shirley Temple a whore? Al had a real passion for her and loved to watch the little girl dance around showing off her panties.

If we can't execute sex offenders, then take their weapons away from them. There is no undoing the damage caused by rape, but you can stop that rapist from raping again by removing his genitals. Rape has everything to do with sex .If it didn't they would use a ball bat instead of a penis. I would rather have been beaten to the floor than forced into sex acts with my own father.

Chapter Thirteen

The Aftermath of the Storm

It is a daily struggle to stay out of the pit my father dug for me as a child. The more pain and misery he causes the more I yearn for revenge. Anyone who has survived abuse by another knows that the memories do not go away, but you can try to use them to your advantage. If you are lucky your abuser was at least arrested and if you're really lucky, he did prison time, but it is far more likely he did not. It is difficult to live in and respect a society that looks the other way for pedophiles and pats your abuser on the back because he goes to church twice a week. You can make it, though and deny him access to your children. Those that rape children do not get to enjoy grandchildren or they shouldn't anyway.

When I think back on our lives I realize that Allan Chadwick was nothing but a criminal who married so that he could have victims for a life time. I wonder what would have happened if he had died in Vietnam or a car wreck? With him gone could we have healed and gone on? All of us could have been more successful that we have been, but it is difficult to override a low self esteem and a cynical attitude. All four of us had above average intelligence and talented in one or more areas. My mother was very nice looking and kind, she could have had anyone, but Al made her feel like she was trapped.

After my mother went through open heart surgery she had a change in attitude. There was much less she tolerated from her husband and his little tricks didn't work anymore. Roses and building car ports did not compensate for his behavior and the crying routine no longer worked. She tried to tell my sister to get back to college and never allow herself to be dependent on a man for her livelihood, that one day she would find herself fifty years old and it will be too late. I know Mom was talking about herself. It was not too late for Mom like she thought and if she had survived the cancer a few years later, I do believe that Al would have had his bags packed. When the fog that Al had spun around his wife finally lifted, it was too late and her only freedom now is on the other side.

I remember the day that Mom had her first appointment with the oncologist. When Al came out he was so excited he could hardly contain himself. There was a delighted glint in his eyes when he announced, "It doesn't look good." I knew then that he was happy that Mom was not going to live. He actually thought that his kids hated their mother as much as he did and we were going to hang out with him. Allan Chadwick and those like him have no souls or they have dead ones. They do not seem to notice or care about the pain they cause. He was cruel to my mother as she went through chemotherapy and she asked that we not leave her alone with him. The weaker Mom became, the meaner Al became and I saw that the old sadistic chickenhawk was still in there.

The last two weeks of Mom's life she spent with a hospital bed in the living room of her house with her sister, Phyllis, there to care for her. I was still working at the prison then and could not be around as much as I wanted to be. I was counting on the recovery time from my knee surgery to spend quality time with Mom and ask her if she was afraid or if there was anything she wanted me to do, but I didn't get the chance. The last night of my mother's life was a hard one. My aunt had called the nurse for oxygen, but it did not show up until hours later. Mom could not breathe and was desperate for ice chips. The nurse had said that Mom would be fine once the oxygen came, so my aunt didn't call anyone in the middle of the night. Phyllis made as much noise as she could busting up ice in the kitchen trying to wake Allan up, but I know he laid in there ignoring the painful scene outside his bedroom door. He did not come out.

The oxygen did not arrive until after seven o'clock when Mom could have used it four hours earlier. By the time my grandmother, me and my sister came over, Mom was comatose. Al was running around looking for his check book. His only concern was having breakfast. It was the blackest day of my life without question and my father was there to make things many times worst as always. Mom finally quit breathing at 9:45 in the morning. I had asked her to let us know when she got to the other side and whether you believe there is an afterlife or not, strange things did happen. The first thing was the terrific thunderstorm that began right when Mom died. She loved to read gothic novels and it could not have been more fitting. That night I thought I saw Mom on my front porch with a bright light behind her. My brain was not used to the fact that Mom was gone, so I thought it was the headlights of her van. She told me that she wasn't going to bother us, that she just wanted to put something inside. When I answered her, she left. The next day I opened the door and found that my keys were in it and I had never left them in the door before. There were big snowflakes falling and covering the trees, which Mom loved. The day of her funeral it was like spring in October.

During the night I had a visit from my grandmother's sister, Ethel Mae, who died in 1949. She told me that Mom was okay because she was there for her. I have to hold onto these things because I cannot bear to think that Mom spent thirty nine years with a monster for nothing. That we all have suffered only to rot in the grave in something unbearable to think.

I cannot change my mother's tragic death or anything that happened to us, but I can tell this story many times over. If one woman out there recognizes herself and gets out of a bad situation, then Mom did not die young for nothing and my brother did not die young for nothing. Pedophiles are dangerous and care for no one, they are not "child lovers" they are child destroyers. It is never too late to escape. Even if you are seventy years old when you get the courage to leave, then go as fast as you can.

Never trust a pedophile with a child. Even if you believe that he has not molested a child for years do not let him around children because they never stop. Never. Your devotion as a wife or partner is not appreciated and when you no longer tow the line or serve your purpose he will treat you accordingly. Going to church does not cure pedophiles and they are not sorry for what they do. Anyone that feels sorry for one is a fool.

It never ceases to amaze me how even when people know what Allan Chadwick is, they dismiss it. The cop next door knew what my father was, yet let his son stay over at Al's unsupervised for long periods of time. When my brother moved over to Al's he did it because he was worried about that little boy. With Mom gone, Al could do as he pleased. It was obvious that the child had made Al's a second home as the kid would just come in when Mark was in the shower or in bed. Mark was in a wheelchair and had a difficult time getting the boy to leave. I did as well because the kid demanded his cookies and candy and had to be physically removed from the house. What does it take to get people to listen when the cops blow you off as well? I can promise you that kid was diddled for his treats and that cop has no one to blame but himself. It was the police that told me and Mark to stop passing out the posters saying Al was a child molester. After all, good old Al has a right to prey on children in peace.

Al tried to put the move on a few old ladies too and they were scared. Some told my aunt they were disturbed by his behavior and would she tell the police? The same women who thought Al could rape them were impressed with the big phony act he put on in church. Did they not notice that when Mom was alive he didn't bother to go? I wrote strong letters to his Sunday school class telling them just what kind of a man Allan Chadwick is because I got sick of people asking me about my poor father and all the tragedy he had to endure. Please, he caused most of it and contributed to all of it. I do not understand those that think church is a cure all. Maybe because I'm Jewish I don't understand. Your actions speak one thousand times louder than declarations of faith. I don't believe that any one else can answer for your sins. If you attend church three times a week and shit on everyone around you I believe your actions cancel out your trips to church.

I do not mean to pick on Christianity, it just disturbs me how many people don't believe what I say about my father because he thumps a Bible once in a while and sheds a few tears. So what? I used to hear the old, "God hates fags" routine from Al all the time. It's funny how people who preach hate only seem to focus on a few little lines in the entire Bible. God thinks women who catch their spouses sexually abusing their children should kill them where they stand. How about that one, Al? Why didn't you ever quote that one to me?

While most ordinary people abhor adult and child rapists, it is very difficult to do anything to them. All a sex offender has to do is point the finger at the victims or whine about his childhood and he walks. Prison is no deterrence, just a stop over so they can rest up for the next round. They cannot be rehabilitated if for no other reason that they do not wish to be. I found a letter that a inmate was sending out to one of his victims. The only reason that this letter was read was the inmate put no stamp on it and he had exceeded his two free letters. When that occurs the letters are opened and read. He was telling her how much he enjoyed their last encounter and what a bitch she was for sending him to prison for an act she wanted. When the inmate got out he was going to pay her another visit and this time she would keep her mouth shut. Yeah, rapists are real sorry for their actions.

There is a convicted pedophile that lives up the street from me. Thanks to Megan's Law I saw him on the Internet, but those too poor to own computers or have Internet service probably will not know about him. I have seen many children playing freely near the man's apartment and I would bet that his neighbors know nothing of his past crimes. How anyone could object to a law that lets the public know predators are among them is beyond my understanding. Silence is truly a lethal weapon for sex offenders who rely on secrecy to continue their reigns of terror. Rapists want to lie like submarines undetected until too late, so they don't want laws that allow people to know who and what they are. They cannot start over again? That's right. That is the whole idea.

Rapists have something fundamentally wrong with them. There is little that distinguishes us from the lower animals and when men force women to mate with them, they cross that boundary. This example is used because that is a real defense that rapists are using today. They are stating that rape is a natural act and they cannot help doing it. The same argument really doesn't hold much water for pedophiles who prefer those children too young to reproduce. My father loves excuses for his behavior and will latch onto to whatever theory exonerates him of wrong doing. Dogs have sex with their own offspring so it must be okay.

This book is a wake up call for everyone. Sex offenders, especially those who target children, are costing society too much. No amount of therapy, support groups, compassion, prison time or love will change them. Enough is enough. Surgical castration is the only solution. Rape is about sex, make no mistake about that one. Pedophiles want sex with children because they find them sexually attractive, not because they are mentally ill. If my father is just some guy who wants to dominate, then he should have just stuck to his fists and threats and left his penis out of it. Children are sexual objects to him and nothing else.

Child sexual and physical abuse causes mental and emotional problems, developmental malfunctions, adult criminals and victim suicide. We need to have zero tolerance for those who use their children to satisfy their own sexual needs. Zero tolerance means surgical castration.

Bob Dole; "I've fallen and I can't get up!"

This was a joke Mark wrote at the hospital just days before he died.

Bibliography

Alleyne, Vanessa. *There Were Times I Thought I was Crazy.* Sister Vision Press, 1999

Allison, Dorothy. *Bastard Out of North Carolina.* New York: Plume 1993

Bass, Ellen and Laura Davis. *The Courage to Heal: A Guide for Women Survivors of Child Sexual Abuse Featuring "Honor the Truth": A Response to the Backlash.* New York: 3rd ed. rev. HarperTrade,1994

Bruni, Frank and Elinor Burkett. *A Gospel of Shame.* New York: Viking Penquin, 1993

Blume, Sue E. *Secret Survivors: Uncovering Incest and Its After Effects in Women.* New York: Ballantine Books, 1997.

Butler, Sandra. *Conspiracy of Silence:The Trauma of Incest.* Volcano Press, Inc., 1996

Case, Joyce and Kathryn Hagans. *When Your Child Has Been Molested: A Parent's Guide to Healing and Recovery.* New York: Jossey-Bass, Inc., 1998

Chadwick, D.A. *Black Capes and Red Bulls.* Lincoln: Writer's Club Press, 2000
God Barks. Lincoln: iuniverse, 2000

Chase, Trudi. When Rabbit Howls. New York: reprint Berkley Publishing Group, 1990

Engel, Beverly. *The Right to Innocence: Healing the Trauma of Childhood Sexual Abuse.* New York: Ballantine Books,

Hamilton, Barbara Small. *The Hidden Legacy: Uncovering, Confronting and Healing Three Generations of Incest.* New York: Cypress House, 2000

Hoyle, Sally. *The Sexualized Child in Foster Care: Assessment and Treatment.* New York: Child Welfare League of America, 2000

Hunter, Mic. Abused Boys: The Neglected Victims of Sexual Abuse. New York: Fawcett Book Group, 1991

Johnson, Janis Tyler. *Mothers of Incest Survivors: Another Side of the Story.* New Albany: Indiana University Press, 1992

Kelly, Pat and Deborah Miller. *Coping with Incest.* New York: Rosen Publishing Group, Inc., 1995

Kesegich, Susan. *Twisted Roots of Evil.* Florida: Twist of Fate Publishing, 1999

Levine, Robert Barry. *When You Are the Partner of a Rape or Incest Survivor: A Workbook for You..*
New York: Resource Publications, 1995

Lew, Mike. *Victims No Longer: Men Recovering From Incest and Other Sexual Child Abuse.* New York: HarperTrade, 1990

Miller, Alice. *Thou Shalt Not Be Aware: Societies Betrayal of the Child.* Trans. Hunter and
Germany: Farrar, Strauss and Giroux, 1998

Myers, John E. *A Mother's Nightmare-Incest: A Practical Legal Guide for Parents and Professionals.* New York: Sage Publications, 1997

Silverman, Sue William. *Because I Remember Terror, Father, I Remember You.* Atlanta: University of Georgia Press, 1999

Strand, Virginia. *Treating Secondary Victims: Intervention with the Non-Offending Mother in the Incest Family.* New York: Sage Publications, 2000

Westerlund, Elaine. *Women's Sexuality After Incest.* New York: W.W. Norton and Company, 1992

Woodson, Jacqueline. I *Hadn't Meant to Tell You This.* New York: Bantam Doubleday, Dell Books for Young Readers, 1995

References

Data for tables obtained from the following government document and the F.B.I. Uniform Crime Reports 1994.

U.S. Department of Justice. Office of Justice Programs, Bureau of Justice Statistics. Jointly Published with the Office of Juvenile Justice and Delinquency Prevention. NCJ-153258 *Child Victimizers: Violent Offenders and Their Victims.* 1996

Rind, Bruce and Philip Tromovitch. "A Meta-analytic Review of Findings from National Samples On Psychological Correlates of Child Sexual Abuse." *Journal of Sex Research* Volume 34, No. 3, (1997) 237-255.

Teicher M.H. et al. "Functional Asymmetry of the of the Temporal Lobes in Young Adults Verbally and Sexually Abused as Children Using fMRI". Department of Psychiatry, Harvard Medical School, Developmental Biopsychiatry Research Program and The Brain Imaging Center, Mclean Hospital, Belmont, MA. 2001

Teicher, M.H. et al. "Cerebellar Vermin Blood Flow: Association with Psychiatric Symptoms in Child Abuse and ADHD". Developmental Biopsychiatry Research Program , Brain Imaging Center, Department of Psychiatry, Harvard Medical School and Mclean Hospital, Belmont, MA 2001

About the Author

D.A. Chadwick has a degree in Criminal Justice and works as a freelance paralegal/researcher in Kansas. She is the author of four other works;

Black Capes and Red Bulls

God Barks

Blatherskites: The Frazer/Gibson Murders

The 1st Field Hospital: The Experiences of T-4 Robert U. Shepard

www.ingramcontent.com/pod-product-compliance
Lightning Source LLC
Chambersburg PA
CBHW061250280526
45784CB00002B/715